EDUCATION AND JOBS

The Center for Urban Education is a private, nonprofit corporation supported in part as a regional educational laboratory by funds from the United States Office of Education, Department of Health, Education, and Welfare. The opinions expressed do not necessarily reflect the position or policy of the Office of Education, and no official endorsement by the Office of Education should be inferred. The Center for Urban Education is located at 105 Madison Avenue, New York, N.Y. 10016.

EDUCATION AND JOBS:
THE
GREAT
TRAINING
ROBBERY

by IVAR BERG

with the assistance
of Sherry Gorelick

Foreword by Eli Ginzberg

BEACON PRESS   BOSTON

Originally published for the Center for Urban Education
by Praeger Publishers
First published as a Beacon Paperback in 1971 by arrangement
with Praeger Publishers
Portions of this publication result from work performed under a contract
with the United States Department of Health, Education, and Welfare,
Office of Education
Beacon Press books are published under the auspices of the
Unitarian Universalist Association
Published simultaneously in Canada by Saunders of Toronto, Ltd.
International Standard Book Number: 0–8070–3181–X
Printed in the United States of America
9 8 7 6 5 4

To Alex Inkeles

Contents

Foreword
by Eli Ginzberg

This foreword has several objectives. First, it will seek to relate Professor Berg's inquiry into the educational requirements for employment to antecedent and current work carried on by the Conservation of Human Resources Project of Columbia University.

Second, it will abstract some of the key findings and policy recommendations of a research investigation that has been under way since 1966, under a subcontract from the Center for Urban Education in New York City, one of the Regional Laboratories of the Office of Education of the United States Department of Health, Education and Welfare. The relations between the Conservation Project and the Center for Urban Education have been cooperative and constructive, and for this we are in debt to Dr. Robert Dentler and Mr. Lawrence Perkins, respectively the Director and the Associate Director for Administration of the Center.

A third objective is to consider a few of the difficult questions that have been precipitated by Professor Berg's investigation and illuminated by his data and theories, but to which he has been unable to present definitive answers. As in every good research undertaking, the problems that are opened up may be even more important than those that are closed out.

During the past decade, much of the effort of the Conservation Project has been focused, not on the disadvantaged, but on the educated and the talented. From these studies we concluded that, while education often provides access to better jobs and better incomes, it offers no guarantee of either. Our investigations also called attention to difficulties that may arise for both the employee and the employer if a man's work requires far less performance than his educational level and his potential would permit. We had earlier concluded that too little education is a disadvantage; apparently, the proposition must be entertained that under certain conditions too much education also can create difficulty.

The studies referred to above were person-centered. They sought to illuminate various aspects of group behavior by analyzing the characteristics and performance of groups. In addition, during the past several years the Conservation Project has carried on a series of investigations into the economic and social institutions that constitute the framework within which people can earn their living:

> *The Pluralistic Economy* (1964)*
> *Electronic Data Processing in New York City* (1966)
> *Manpower and the Growth of Producer Services* (1967)
> *Manpower Strategy for the Metropolis* (1968)
> *The Process of Work Establishment* (1969)
> *The Peripheral Worker* (1969)
> *Allied Health Manpower: Trends and Prospects* (1969)
> *The Hard-to-Employ in Western Europe: Policies and Programs* (1970)

The thrust of these investigations was to emphasize the extent to which the American economy is being transformed in focus from the production of goods to the production of services, and the ever-larger role of the not-for-profit sector (government and nonprofit institutions); the wide range in

---

* Published by McGraw-Hill. All the other books listed are published by the Columbia University Press.

the educational and other characteristics of people employed in the service sector; the extent to which new industries are able and willing to tap sources of labor supply irrespective of formal qualifications; the subtle and not-so-subtle competition for jobs between white women and Negroes; the way in which employer practices in hiring, assignment, and promotion help to shape the labor market; and the striking differences between the United States and Western Europe in making room for the disadvantaged, including the poorly educated.

While these several investigations of the Conservation Project were under way, directed toward deepening our understanding of the workings of the labor market so that we would no longer have to rely on a model at once too simple and too rigid, public leaders and academic economists were giving birth to a new ideology. They proclaimed that the key to economic development is liberal expenditures for education, which, by improving the quality of labor, are the heart of productivity increases. From the President down, the leadership proclaimed throughout the land: "Education pays; stay in school." The economists calculated to a fraction of a per cent the extent to which education pays.

Professor Berg, by temperament a skeptic, by training a sociologist, and by choice a student of manpower, found the new orthodoxy neither intellectually compelling nor emotionally satisfying. He therefore set out to study the relations of education to employment, in part by collecting new data, in part by critically reviewing the principal empirical studies that had earlier been concerned with this theme.

Here are some of the important findings that emerge from his study. Professor Berg begins by stressing the bias inherent in American life and thought that makes us look at a malfunctioning of the labor market in terms of the personal failings of workers in search of jobs. What is more reasonable than to postulate that if only these workers had more education and training they would not be unemployed or under-employed?

Reasonable, yes—but not necessarily right. Among his incisive analyses is Professor Berg's critique of the conventional wisdom of researchers who have elaborated the "human capital" approach. These academics have adduced evidence suggesting that the return on investment in people is greater than the average return on other forms of investment. But Professor Berg correctly cautions that one must not be caught in circular reasoning. The critical point is not whether men and women who complete high school or college are able subsequently to earn more than those who don't, but whether their higher earnings are a reflection of better performance as a result of more education or training or of factors other than the diplomas and degrees they have acquired.

In Professor Berg's terms, perhaps the key to the puzzle is not what education contributes to an individual's productivity but how it helps him to get a better-paying job in the first place. He is careful not to challenge the "human capital" economists on the narrow ground that their calculations are faulty or that they fail to support their conclusion that "education pays"; rather, he focuses on the reality that underlies their tenet. To prove their case, Professor Berg argues, they would have to study education in relation to the intervening variable of productivity rather than jump over it and deal only with income. To bring the point home sharply, I have often asked my students at Columbia's Graduate School of Business why a leading company is willing to pay them, when they graduate, $11,000 to $12,000 annually to sell soap or breakfast foods. Why do large companies offer such handsome salaries to beginners, even those with M.A.'s? The trouble with the argument offered by "human capital" theorists may be that it is a rational explanation of behavior that is largely irrational.

One of the interesting statistical exercises in which Professor

Berg engaged was to recalculate with care the large body of data assembled by the United States Department of Labor about workers' characteristics and employers' requirements, to determine the nature and extent of changes in skills required over time in comparison with changes in the educational preparation of the American working population. His most critical finding is that with the passage of time there has been a tendency for a larger group of persons to be in jobs that utilize less education than they have. If this is a valid conclusion from the admittedly rough data, it suggests the need for caution in propagating the nostrum that more education is the answer to the nation's problems.

Educational requirements for employment continue to rise. Employers are convinced that, by raising their demands, they will be more likely to recruit an ambitious, disciplined work force that will be more productive than workers who have terminated their schooling earlier. Professor Berg's principal analyses are directed to this central line. His conclusions fail to support employer practices and convictions. First, he reemphasizes the point made by many students about the wide range in education and other characteristics of workers in the same job category—that is, workers who do the same work and earn the same wages. Next, he finds that in certain areas, such as the selling of insurance, workers with less education but more experience perform better and earn more. This is hardly surprising, since the skill involved is modest and education is irrelevant beyond a qualifying level. Nevertheless, the enthusiasts of education continue to press for higher qualifications without reference to the task to be performed or the environment in which the work is to be carried out.

Many employers seek to justify their high educational demands by reference to the need for promoting workers into higher ranks, where their education *will* be needed. But Professor Berg makes two telling points. In many companies only a small percentage of those who are hired are ever promoted to such positions. Further, the more highly qualified are often no longer in the company when the opportunity for promotion arises. Their frustration with work that does not fully utilize their educational background leads them to seek jobs elsewhere.

Professor Berg demonstrates, by reference to the ways in which schoolteachers receive higher compensation, the illogic of the "education craze." Teachers who take additional courses in order to earn salary increments eventually catapult themselves out of the teaching arena, since they finally are "overeducated" for classroom work.

Among the largest and most revealing bodies of data that Professor Berg selects to review critically are those that he obtained from the armed services and the federal civil service. His findings are unequivocal. In every instance, the data prove overwhelmingly that the critical determinants of performance are not increased educational achievement but other personality characteristics and environmental conditions.

On the policy front, Professor Berg is cautious and constrained despite his devastating attack on the errors in contemporary thought and action which hold that education is the open sesame to economic wellbeing. Specifically, he argues in favor of upgrading many of the "overeducated" who now fill positions in the middle ranks into the less crowded upper-level jobs and at the same time upgrading those at the bottom so that they could advance into middle-level positions. The hard-to-employ could then be fitted into the lower-level jobs. This is directly in line with the recommendations made early in 1968 by the National Manpower Advisory Committee to the Secretaries of Labor and HEW Manpower Programs.

The final implication of Professor Berg's analysis is for policy-makers to focus much more on actions aimed at increasing the demand for labor. If there is a shortfall in demand—and the federal estimate places about 11 million persons in subemployment categories—then indeed, changing the characteristics of workers by adding to their schooling cannot be *the* answer.

But trenchant as is Professor Berg's treatment of the conventional wisdom, he has had to leave certain critical issues in suspense. They should, however, be briefly noted.

The question of how enlarged efforts on the educational front are specifically connected to increasing productivity of the economy finds no answer in his book—or in the books of the many economists who have addressed themselves specifically to this issue. No one doubts that a linkage exists, but its nature remains obscure. Will economic expansion best be speeded by reducing the proportion of illiterates, improving graduate training, making certain that women are educated to their full potential, raising the level of vocational education? All these questions suggest more education, but it remains to be demonstrated just how doing more on one or all of these fronts is related to accelerating economic growth.

Another subject that has yet to be confronted sharply and clearly is the relation of education to employment from the vantage point of qualifying rather than optimal considerations. Again, few students would deny that minimal levels of educational achievement have distinct relevance, although the concept of the optimum remains to be delineated.

A third tantalizing subject, with which the author deals in passing, relates to the place of education in selection for the entrance job versus its role as a screening factor for career progression. Failure to consider future positions in initial screening is an error matched only by neglect of the consequences of having a surplus of "overqualified" persons on the staff, all waiting for advancement.

Other problems that are touched upon but not considered in depth include the relative return on investment in educational effort before and after a man enters employment. In what fields of endeavor is the level of education likely to be of determining importance in performance, and in what fields is it likely to be only indirectly related to output? How can the circularity of current "rate of return" analyses be broken into so that more meaningful findings can emerge about the relations of education, productivity, and earnings? To what extent is education a surrogate for other qualities that are predictive of a higher level of eventual performance? What are the dangers of gearing wage increments to educational accomplishments?

A book that helps to illuminate a large number of important issues, even while forced to bypass others, provides the reader with rich fare. In addition, Professor Berg has opened up important new questions and has cast serious doubts upon accepted answers to old questions that most Americans had long believed were beyond discussion. In attacking the hallowed beliefs of statesmen, employers, economists, and educators, he has let in new light where light has long been needed. And he has done so with scholarly acumen, stylistic grace, and a saving sense of humor—qualities all too rare in academe.

Preface and Acknowledgments

It gives an educator no pleasure to present the materials in this volume. As they stand, these materials will discourage both those with lofty conceptions of what education could be and those of a more practical bent who see no fundamental inconsistency between a highly principled and a highly pragmatic stance concerning education in America.

The researcher, of course, has some obligation to comment on his findings, and I have done so in selecting the book's subtitle and in the concluding chapter. It has saddened me that the data adumbrated in the research process did not inspire a more optimistic reaction; the times are sufficiently out of joint without adding the independent weight of the scientist's tables and statistics to the gloom prevailing among thoughtful Americans. It is particularly distressing to appear to launch what some will construe, mistakenly, to be an "attack" on education in its present beleaguered state. Surely there is a distinction between an effort to confront widespread and rather uncritical ideas about education with relevant data, on the one hand, and an anti-intellectual attack, on the other. The careful reader will, meanwhile, forgive a measure of despondency in an author whose science is tempered by an occasional self-indulgent expression of his feelings.

My feelings toward the research enterprise as such are less complex. It enabled me to work with many people, and, if the results of that work are distressing, the work itself was an unqualified pleasure. Sherry Gorelick, now a doctoral candidate in Columbia University's Department of Sociology, has been a creative and stimulating colleague from the outset. She more than repaid my confidence in her innumerable capabilities. Marcia K. Freedman was a constant benefactor, and it is a pleasure to acknowledge the fact in general terms. Her specific contributions are noted in appropriate contexts, but these do no justice to her role as collaborator in the best sense of the word. Gretchen Maclachlan helped at all stages of the study and inventively adapted esoteric data-processing techniques to a number of the blocks of data.

Several distinguished colleagues have read drafts of the manuscript and given abundantly of their very limited time. Among them are Professors Giulio Pontecorvo, James W. Kuhn, and Maurice Wilkinson, of Columbia University's Graduate School of Business. These gentlemen made detailed comments and gave much helpful technical advice. Professor S. M. Miller, of New York University, also gave generously of advice and, in a way, helped to bring about the research effort by his encouragement before the formal study ever began. Edward Robie, of the Equitable Life Assurance Company, was most generous in offering comments after a close reading of the document. Professor David Rogers, of New York University, read a very early draft and made many valuable suggestions, as did Professor Robert Dreeben, of the University of Chicago. None of these readers bear any responsibility, however, for the formulations or interpretations contained in the report.

I am especially pleased to acknowledge the thoughtful comments of Louis Hacker, Emeritus Professor of History at Columbia. This indefatigable scholar, with endless patience and extraordinary erudition, is a model intellectual. I am richer for having made his acquaintance and will recall this enterprise as the happy excuse that brought us together.

Robert Dentler, Director of the Center for Urban Education, and his staff have been helpful at all points. Professor

Dentler's generous views toward the original project and the Center's support facilitated my work to a most significant degree. The fact that he never once sought to influence the study in any way speaks more than a little for this scholar's sensitivity to the nature of research. In the same context, I am happy to acknowledge the support of the Faculty Research Review Committee of the Columbia Business School; its members were more than tolerant.

I am grateful, too, for a sabbatical leave from Columbia during the academic year 1966–67; Deans Courtney Brown and Garland C. Owens, with the then Provost of the University, Jacques Barzun, arranged for the details of my association with the Center for Urban Education to be appropriately folded into my Columbia University obligations during that valuable year.

Thanks must also go to many students and colleagues who patiently listened to me during the long period in which I was "fixated" on my work. I must have bored them often indeed, but they never acknowledged that.

Finally, it is a pleasure to acknowledge the valuable help rendered by Ruth Szold Ginzberg in her thorough review of the final draft of the book; she facilitated the movement from typescript to book by her careful and graceful work. At the final stage I am the beneficiary of Gladys Topkis, of Praeger, whose enthusiastic guidance has made my relationship with my publisher a most agreeable one.

It is impossible to properly acknowledge Eli Ginzberg's many important roles in my life as colleague and friend. He has been a constant source of delight and support. It is similarly impossible to express my gratitude to my wife; among other things, she saw me through a series of personal tragedies at the study's outset and, thereby, made so many things possible.

The dedication to Alex Inkeles, of Harvard University, reflects, in part, the fact that I had trouble with a question he raised in 1957; psychologists refer to the phenomenon as the Ziegarnik Effect. It required an entire book to be liberated from the enduring sense of "task incompletion."

IVAR BERG

New York City
November, 1969

EDUCATION AND JOBS

I Educational Commitments: An Overview

Few other topics enjoy the favored place accorded education on the contemporary American agenda of public concerns—a reflection of the "academocracy" we have become. There are almost as many people attending school full time in America as there are working in full-time occupations. Today 99 per cent of all eligible preteen children are in school; as recently as 1910 there were nearly two million employed youngsters aged 7–13.

No matter what statistics are charted to measure America's educational commitments, the direction is up and the magnitudes are increasing. In 1950, 59 per cent of all persons 17 years or older had graduated from high school; by 1964 the figure was 76.3 per cent. Americans spent $9 billion on education in 1950, $29 billion in 1963, and nearly $49 billion in 1966–67. In 1956, some 309,000 Americans earned college degrees, compared to 500,000 in 1964. And whereas slightly more than 20 per cent of the students who completed fifth grade in 1944 went on to college, more than 40 per cent of fifth-graders in 1957 eventually entered college, a remarkably high "school retention" figure.

The public has become education-conscious to an extraordinary degree, a fact that helps to explain the considerable rise in the educational attainments of the work force and the boom in what has been termed, somewhat infelicitously, the knowledge or education industry. The well-publicized concern of parents, young people, and a variety of social commentators with education and academic performance is more than matched by the concern of researchers, educators, government policy-makers, and businessmen. Thus we note a phenomenal increase in interest in education—that is, in schooling and related training programs—among economists, manpower experts, foreign-aid officials, marketing specialists, publishers, and even investment analysts in the nation's financial centers. In each of these circles, education, generally equated with years of formal schooling, is seen as a major factor affecting productivity, economic growth, income shares, and the array of other phenomena that corporations consider in decisions regarding plant location, advertising, and production planning. But the possibility that there may *not* be a considerable disparity between the educational achievements of the American work force and the educational requirements for a significant proportion of jobs—a possibility explored in this book—has been ignored.

Sociologists, of course, have traditionally regarded education as among the crucial influences affecting the rates of everything from social mobility to social pathology. In a task-force report of the President's Crime Commission, two sociologists mobilized data suggesting that juvenile delinquency is linked to school failure and to shortcomings in the response of the educational establishment to the challenge that such failure poses.[1]

The "education craze" in America has resulted from a number of overlapping though distinguishable sets of forces. Although it is not possible to assign weights or even precise chronological priorities to these forces, they deserve mention here since many of them have helped to shape the correlates

---

[1] Walter E. Schafer and Kenneth Polk, "Delinquency and the Schools," *Juvenile Delinquency and Youth Crime* (Washington: President's Commission on Law Enforcement and Administration of Justice, 1957), pp. 222-27.

that this study undertakes to identify and examine; they have helped to generate the commitments regularly translated into massive expenditures for education and into the increasing educational achievements of the American people.[2]

Our commitment to education is, in historical perspective, well established. America has no feudal tradition, a fact that Karl Marx counted as significant in appraising the character of social classes in America; for example, there has been no systematic effort on the part of the "haves" in this country to counter the interests of other citizens in developing a public school system.

The support given the school system by particular groups, of course, has not been entirely free of class and class-related values; the content of public (as well as private) education that benefits from the political and financial backing of a pluralistic society understandably reflects the many bends and twists in the ideologies of the groups of which this pluralism is composed. Although class politics cannot be divorced from American education in its development, such politics did not have a simple negative effect; rather, it helps to explain both our commitment to education in general and the disparities among the components of our educational system.[3] Our class structure has thus been part of the pluralistic system in which ethnic, racial, religious, and other affiliations have shaped people's and groups' wishes and choices in such ways that the politics of status has cut across the politics of class.

The nineteenth-century frontier, with some of the "safety valve" effects imputed to it by the historian Frederick Jack-

[2] For present purposes "educational achievement" refers to years of formal schooling completed. Educational achievement in other places and times will be explored later in this chapter.

[3] For an overview, see Lawrence A. Cremin, *The Transformation of the School* (New York: Random House, Vintage Books, 1964). The best picture of present-day commitments to American education can be found in Solon T. Kimball and James E. McClellan, Jr., *Education and the New America* (New York: Random House, 1962).

son Turner, reduced the pressures on the population to see education as the one means to economic wellbeing. At the same time, it helped to reduce the potential for conflict among classes that were more clearly delineated than they were before the turn of that century. As a consequence of ethnic, regional, and other differences, debates over education were often of a different order than would have been predictable in a society of elites contending with a volatile population constrained in their economic circumstances by limited educational opportunities.[4]

The predominant reaction of Americans to the Great Depression of the 1930's provides another clue to evolving conceptions of education in America. The reports of such sensitive scholars as E. Wight Bakke, of Yale University, brought home the fact that Americans had learned well the importance of education in a society that had become highly industrialized. Bakke documented what many suspected; namely, that, by and large, unemployed Americans were more likely to blame themselves than the "system" for their unhappy circumstances in those bitter years.

Among the causes of misery regularly identified by Bakke's respondents were their shortsighted decisions to seek income over educational achievement during the boom of the '20's. Many of them stated that they were more likely to have had depression-proof jobs had they been willing to defer the gratifications that they expected to achieve by entering the labor force in favor of continuing or completing their education.[5] No one can estimate how much of the educational achievement of the population aged 40–50 today is attributable to the economic pressures generated in the "dirty

[4] For an interesting analysis of splits within a large Norwegian-American group over the common school, religious instruction, and language training, see Nicholas Tavuchis, *Pastors and Immigrants* (The Hague: Martinus Nijhoff, 1963).

[5] E. Wight Bakke, *The Unemployed Worker* and *Citizens Without Work* (New Haven: Yale University Press, 1940).

thirties" and perceived directly by them or transmitted to them by their parents.

Laws of the late depression period restricting the labor-force participation of youths gave added impetus to the role of education; almost by default, education assumed an increasingly important place as a result of the new limitation on young people's working established in child-labor legislation. In a bizarre manifestation of Parkinson's Law, education expanded to fill the time of many youths whose social roles had been redesigned by the several state legislatures, with diminished opposition from the courts, and by the 1938 Fair Labor Standards Act.[6]

Historical commitments, depression-born experiences, and the discontinuities in traditional social arrangements decreed by lawmakers thus provided a necessary cultural base for the emergence of new popular attitudes toward education. The needs of the World War II period subsequently drove home additional lessons about the significance and potential of education, as America adapted institutions and attitudes to the exigencies of international conflict.

Wartime productivity gains in the domestic economy and the successes of our military forces were, to a considerable degree, related reflections of the capacity of Americans to train and educate large masses of people in a relatively short time. That the members of a "civilian" Army (and Navy) should be rewarded for their sacrifices by subsidized educational and training opportunities (the "G.I. Bill") reflected the nation's implicit acknowledgment of the importance of education and training even as it sought a way to express its gratitude to returning servicemen and women. Screening programs, con-

---

[6] A federal child-labor law, the Keating-Owen Act, was passed by Congress in 1916 but was declared unconstitutional in 1918. A similar act of 1919 was declared unconstitutional in 1922. The Child Labor Amendment to the Constitution was submitted to the states for ratification in 1924; by 1950, only 26 of the necessary 36 states had ratified it.

ducted in connection with the needs of the War Department during World War I, had already indicated some of the manpower losses that accrue to a society through inadequacies in its educational programs. Such losses, reconfirmed by the rejection figures of the Selective Service System in the '50's and '60's, have strengthened arguments that a great deal of training must be undertaken to satisfy America's defense requirements, even if there were no substantial benefits to individuals or to the economy to be derived from public policies to "upgrade" the intellectual-educational achievements of "disadvantaged" Americans.

Education and the Postwar Years

The Employment Act of 1946 spelled out the federal government's responsibility for economic planning and research and virtually guaranteed education a place in the forefront of public-policy concerns. Despite events during the worst years of the Cold War and the tight labor market of the postwar era, interest in education continued to grow; after all, during the early postwar years the population move to the nation's suburbs took on boom proportions. This movement was caught up almost immediately with concerns about the educational dollar. The facts of population growth, technological changes, and the upgrading of job requirements also guaranteed continuing cumulative commitments favoring education.

The place of education in popular thinking was nowhere better illustrated than in the apparent indifference and therefore approval with which the American people responded to the policy that gave large numbers of college students deferments from military service during the Korean War. With almost no opposition, defense manpower planners Anna Rosenberg and John Hannah, the latter a college president, were able to encumber a democracy with the strange idea that "brainpower" must be liberated from the military obligations facing the many thousands of World War II veterans who were recalled as reservists to fight in Korea and the hundreds of thousands of younger men for whom college was not a likely prospect. This concept, which has enjoyed Congressional support, has continued to inform Selective Service policy during the war in Vietnam.

The launching of Sputnik in 1957 and the attendant successes of the Soviet scientific establishment spotlighted education in America as never before. Critics of American education capitalized on this highly sophisticated scientific achievement of a rival power to stir deep American anxieties about the state of education. Admiral Rickover's battles with those of his fellow officers who had been notably unenthusiastic about the role of nuclear technology in the United States Navy were featured in news columns, and comparisons were drawn between Soviet and American educational programs, to the disadvantage of the latter. Indeed, an obscure Harvard graduate student who had written a book on Soviet professional education a year before Sputnik[7] became a national figure overnight when he interrupted his doctoral studies for a televised interview with the late Edward R. Murrow, in which these comparisons were reviewed. Although it is nonsensical to believe that Sputnik "caused" the current excitement, it does seem that the orbiting packages of Soviet scientific and technological achievements, together with East-West tensions, provided the necessary impetus to move a host of issues surrounding American education to stage center. Most knowledgeable observers, for example, would credit the National Defense Education Act of 1958 to Sputnik.

A revolution with respect to research and development in

[7] Nicholas DeWitt, *Soviet Professional Manpower: Its Education, Training and Supply* (Washington: National Science Foundation, 1955).

America, of course, was already under way before the advent of Sputnik; reports had appeared with increasing frequency concerning alleged shortages of engineering and scientific personnel. Business leaders, meanwhile, were paying technicians starting salaries of a magnitude that reflected manpower shortages in industry. The growth of defense industries, the beginning domestication of computer technology, and the enormous strides of the electronics industry had contributed significantly to the growing demands for "educated manpower."

In the period after the Korean War, before we became parties to a space race, it was already apparent that the outcome of our contest with the Soviet Union would not be unrelated to developments in the American economy. Recognition of this fact, during a time when the economy was sluggish, generated a prolonged debate about the conditions necessary for increasing the rate of economic growth. Although this problem had interested professional social scientists concerned with European recovery and, later, those concerned with the "developing nations" of Africa, Latin America, and Asia, the role of education in national economies had not been considered systematically before the mid-1950's.

It was perhaps in connection with this problem of growth that education received its biggest boost since Sputnik. This boost, inevitably, was reflected in the work of economists. In a widely heralded effort to delineate the contribution of various factors to economic growth, Edward Denison, of the Brookings Institution, reported his estimates that education accounted for 23 per cent of the growth in total national income and 42 per cent of the growth in per capita income in the United States from 1929 to 1957.[8] His figures were remarkably close to those in the landmark study published in

[8] Edward F. Denison, *The Sources of Economic Growth in the United States and the Alternatives Before Us* (New York: Committee on Economic Development, 1962).

the same year by Theodore Schultz, of the University of Chicago.[9]

These studies and others by Schultz and Denison, together with studies of the "rate of return" on investments in "human capital" by Gary Becker (1962 and 1965), Jacob Mincer (1962), Fritz Machlup (1962), and related investigations by Weisbrod, Hansen, and others[10] have almost persuaded economists to consider "improvements in the quality of human resources as one of the major sources of economic growth."[11] These conclusions, which are examined in Chapter II, confirm the assumption of most sociologists that education is one of the most significant characteristics of American social structure.

Since students in these two disciplines assigned such enormous weight to education in their studies of economic growth and social mobility, it is hardly surprising that their views found expression in the policies of a government responsive to intellectuals in general and social scientists in particular. President Kennedy's design for his war on poverty especially gave considerable weight to programs calculated to remedy the individual and personal deficiencies of the poor and unemployed. These deficiencies were defined, in large part, as shortcomings in the educational backgrounds of low-income groups, shortcomings that had to be eliminated in order that the "other America" might find work in an economy that by 1962 was beginning to quicken its pace.

The idea fell on willing ears in a society that accepted a mechanistic interpretation of the relationship between education and employment. If jobs require increasing educational

[9] Theodore W. Schultz, "Reflections on Investment in Man," Supplement, Oct., 1962, "Investment in Human Beings," *Journal of Political Economy*, LXX, Part 2 (1962), 1–8.
[10] See Mary Jean Bowman, "The Human Investment Revolution in Economic Thought," *Sociology of Education*, XXXIX (1966), 111–37, for a convenient summary and detailed citations.
[11] Schultz, *op. cit.*, p. 3.

achievements, and if the society provides opportunities for education, then, according to the sapient orthodoxy, the burden falls upon the individual to achieve the education necessary for employment.

On the face of it, such logic is not vulnerable to much criticism. Difficulties arise, however, if "educational opportunities" are not truly available, without restriction, to all. Difficulties also arise if the quality of education is not uniform and if, as a consequence of variations, some groups encounter education in a way that diminishes rather than reinforces the urge to pursue academic achievement.

For all its advantages, the war on poverty in its first years has had little impact on urban schools in low-income areas, where young people have dismal encounters with the learning enterprise. Nor has the "war" substantially affected the distribution of American wealth in ways that facilitate the formation of positive attitudes among low-income people toward their children's schools or educational experiences. Nevertheless, it has become accepted doctrine that education is an important answer to many of the questions that emerged when the "other America" was discovered on the "new frontier" by the builders of the "great society."

The emphasis on education in the war against poverty was not entirely naive, as the preceding paragraph might imply, nor was it entirely misplaced. Changes in the occupational structure of the American economy cannot be gainsaid by pointing to the oversimplifications in programs that do not create jobs in proportion to population increases, or that fail to educate large numbers of urban youths. Thus, while America fools many of its young by linking job opportunities to diplomas and degrees from schools that provide sometimes pitifully inadequate—indeed, appalling—experiences, the demand for a better-educated work force has grown in relation to changes in the mix of occupations accompanying technological and other changes in American industry.

These changes, which are considered in Chapter III, undoubtedly help to account for the changing educational requirements for jobs. Employers, particularly in the private sector, are generally committed to the position that it is entirely sensible to keep raising their educational requirements. By so doing they have contributed significantly to the concerns about education already discussed. The fact that education has also become a profitable area for business enterprise both reflects and feeds the surges of interest embodied in popular debate and public policy concerning education.

Education, in fine, has become a big issue. The events, problems, and assessments of the post-World War II era have seemingly confirmed the relevance of education in a society in which education was, early, a valued component of its cultural base. Our democratic commitments give ideological support to the proposition that an educated population is an informed population, better equipped to govern itself through judicious appraisals of public issues. Our commitments to cultural traditions, such as they are, give additional impetus to the expansion of facilities in which creativity and sensitivity are nurtured. Our commitment to pragmatism assures a place for education as the instrument by which utilitarian values are most rationally transmitted. Our concern—at least the concern of most Americans—that Americans share a political ethos guarantees schools a sanctified place in the hierarchy of institutions in which the imperatives of citizenship and other tribal values may be transmitted.

The Present Research Problem

In most assessments of the benefits and "returns" accruing to America and its citizens from education, there has been a distinct bias in favor of the assumptions, logic, and methods of the economist. However, although a method that employs dollar values may reveal some of the elements in the story, it does not make room for other correlates of education to which pecuniary value are not easily attached. The present investigation was undertaken specifically to identify some of these correlates.

As was noted earlier, employers are among the groups contributing to the current emphasis on education, and, since job opportunities are so intimately linked with the wellbeing of our citizens, employers' use of educational requirements in the labor market becomes strategically important. It is their behavior and the consequences of their behavior upon which the present research focuses.

Analyses which examine the benefits of education tend to consider only income and related returns and to define costs in narrow terms. Employers have been inclined to accept a parallel logic without much question in the administration of wages and salaries, believing in general that better-educated employees will be better for their organizations. According to managers in private enterprise, educational achievements have been taken as evidence of self-discipline and potential for promotion. Moreover, trainability is presumed to correlate with educational achievement, as are productivity, personality —important in many jobs—and adaptability.

When employers' assessments are combined with the careful accounting calculations of economists and the findings of sociologists that increased education is associated with "better" social values and child-rearing practices, the case for education seems buttressed indeed. However, the bearing of education upon the numerous problems that perturb employers and, when given publicity, other interested observers has not been examined.

In this study such problems as turnover, productivity, and worker dissatisfaction are considered in conjunction with the educational achievements of workers in a large number of occupations, at the upper as well as the lower end of the skill hierarchy, in a broad array of organizations, both public and private.

It is not easy to put a price tag on worker dissatisfaction, nor is it easy to evaluate quantitatively the net gains and losses to employers and to the "system" that accrue from worker turnover and other aspects of personnel policy. Nevertheless, the case for investments in education[12] and for upgrading educational requirements in personnel-selection procedures is not complete until a broader analysis of costs in the world of work has been developed and applied. Aggregated data on productivity and income in their relation to education tell us little of the "effects" of education in a given occupational setting and in the attitudes of workers. Moreover, the assumptions of employers concerning the alleged superiorities of better-educated employees are no substitutes for data demonstrating their validity.

To broaden the concept of costs and returns and to give a fuller picture than can be drawn with the economist's mathematical reconstructions, it is necessary to back away from gross data on earnings and consider other aspects of employee performance, including productivity. To test the assumptions of employers, it is necessary to examine both the data they collect about their employees and relevant data collected from representative samples of workers outside their employ.

The specific steps undertaken in the research will be explained in the chapters that follow, but the main lines of the investigation can be outlined here:

The argument presented by proponents of the general increase in educational requirements rests in part on the assumption that jobs themselves have changed in such a way that

---

[12] We are leaving aside the "consumption" value of education to individuals and society; in this study our goal is more modest—to extend the lines of analysis staked out by economists in this area and join them in begging the interesting question bearing on the cultural, political, and psychological benefits associated with education.

they require workers with higher educational achievements than were required of workers who performed similar jobs in an earlier time period. In this argument, of course, technological changes that have contributed to this state of affairs are singled out in support. However, it is not easy to assess the effects of technological change.[13] An attempt to survey the changes in "actual" educational requirements between 1936 and 1966, based on careful job studies by field representatives of the United States Employment Service, proved impossible to complete because of discontinuities in sampling procedures from 1936 to 1957. Had such longitudinal analysis been possible, the effects of the size of the labor market and of technological changes could have been examined with some degree of confidence, since these job descriptions are highly detailed, and since data on employment rates over time do capture changes fairly well, however inadequate they may be to describe a given period.

It *was* possible, however, to examine the educational requirements for about 4,000 jobs whose "constituent parts" had been examined systematically in 1957 *and* in 1965, and for which educational and training requirements were meaningfully estimated for both periods. These data, adjusted so that they could be used in conjunction with census reports on the educational achievements of the work force by occupation, have made it possible to estimate the relationship of "real" educational requirements for jobs to the educational achievements of the American labor force.[14] In Chapter III the mechanics of this laborious enterprise are reported, together with the conclusion that since "achievements" appear to have exceeded requirements in most job categories, it cannot be argued helpfully that technological and related changes attending most

[13] For a brief, lucid, and relevant discussion, see Robert M. Solow, "Technology and Unemployment," *The Public Interest*, No. 1 (1965), 17–26.

[14] Such an analysis was first attempted in 1962, by R. S. Eckaus, of the Massachusetts Institute of Technology. See Chapter II, below.

jobs account for the pattern whereby better-educated personnel are "required" and utilized by managers.

In the face of these findings, we will examine in detail the
reasons managers give in defense of educational requirements
for employee selection, with special reference to job categories
for which educational requirements have been raised in recent
years. In Chapter IV these reasons are reported as they were
gleaned from interviews with employers in the packaging,
steel, rubber, textile, and other industries. In most industries
the employers sought to justify the decision to use education as
a "screening device" by claiming that educational achievement
is evidence of an ability to get along with others and to make
the most of opportunities. They also made reference to the
greater potential of better-educated workers for promotion
to higher-paying, more skilled and responsible jobs.

However, when efforts were made to pinpoint the ways in
which "better-educated" workers prove to be superior to those
with less formal education, it was discovered that business
firms typically do not collect data that would make such
comparisons possible. Where relevant data are available—for
example, on such matters as grievance patterns, turnover, productivity, absenteeism, and worker attitudes—they are rarely
analyzed as a means of discovering the validity of *any* selection procedure or screening device. The argument of employers that "information costs are high" must be weighed
against the facts that computer technology has made personnel
studies increasingly easy and that manpower costs are among
the largest expenses facing most enterprises.

Assessment of the data in the next three chapters suggests
the need for consolidating from other sources the parts of the
puzzle they help to define. Chapters V–VIII accordingly report our efforts to specify the relationships between educational achievement and workers' performance on the basis of
(1) published materials that typically deal with the work performance of employees in middle- and low-level occupations;

(2) a secondary analysis of data on white-collar workers in each of several firms; and (3) original studies of a variety of employees in an insurance company, a large metropolitan bank, a national news magazine, the eight branch plants of a Southern textile company, and a paper-manufacturing company.

The conclusions do not give much comfort to those who argue that educational requirements serve managers well as a screening device with respect to either potential or actual performance.

Since managers frequently point to the importance of hiring "promotable" employees, it is useful and relevant to consider whether employees in diverse employment settings go up the ladder of occupational success more rapidly as they are better educated. The results of an examination of employees' careers in a large urban telephone company, an urban power company, six electrical manufacturing companies, and at the middle levels of a large company in the electronics field indicate that organizational careers are a function of loyalty, longevity, and a certain managerial capacity to splinter the skills of others into diverse vertical categories that exhibit nominal rather than real differences. Except at higher levels (engineers and scientists), educational differences tend to wash out among employees at any organizational level. These findings, reported in Chapter V, illuminate those reported in a later chapter, that frequency of turnover is positively related to education.

Since better-educated workers have higher turnover rates, an organization is often obliged to promote substantial numbers of employees regardless of their educational achievements and regardless of the employer's "bias" in favor of education as a screening device. Sometimes managers are surprised to learn of the relationships between education and turnover, as in one company in which managers reported that the better-educated technicians in their employ were the "best" technicians. As the data from his company will show, the less educated technicians received higher evaluations from supervisors and had longer service than technicians with higher educational achievements in comparable jobs; the managers, however, assumed that these "better" employees had completed more years of schooling!

An assessment of education in its relation to worker attitudes is a risky enterprise, for we do not know what mixture of favorable and unfavorable work attitudes is optimal for the firm, for the individual or for our industrial society. It is hard to believe that worker discontent necessarily detracts from ambition or that satisfaction contributes to productivity. The literature in this realm of sociological interest could be selectively cited to prove almost anything.[15]

In general, however, managers spend considerable sums of money on worker surveys, personnel programs, sensitivity training for leaders, work benefits, and other efforts to improve employee morale. The relevant question, therefore, may well be whether these practices are not in large measure designed to undo the demoralizing effects of hiring policies that stress education. In light of the current concern with employee "morale," it was logical to re-examine published studies of worker satisfaction and to undertake secondary analyses of studies in which available data pertaining to the attitudinal correlates of education had not been exploited.

The data from both types of analysis reveal that education is more often than not an important factor accounting for dissatisfaction among workers in many occupational categories and is related to dissatisfaction in a considerable variety of work experiences and employer policies. Chapters VI and VII, which present the relevant results, support the conclusion that managers who raise educational requirements are likely to

[15] See the widely cited discussion of this problem in Harold L. Wilensky, "Human Relations in the Workplace: An Appraisal of Some Recent Research," in Conrad Arensberg *et al.*, eds., *Research in Industrial Human Relations* (New York: Harper, 1957), pp. 25-50.

purchase for themselves some, if not all, of the very dissatisfactions that their expensive personnel practices are calculated to reduce.

The increasing numbers of employees in the public sector make it most desirable to consider data from this population as well. Data on the career experiences of a 5-per-cent sample of nearly 200,000 federal civil servants, which were only partially exploited before the present investigation, are examined in Chapter VIII, as are relevant data on the Federal Aviation Agency; they seem to reveal somewhat more judicious recruiting and assignment practices than obtain in the private sector. Data on the performance of military personnel in technical and other schools support the assertion that there are better predictors of the learning and "trainability" capabilities of personnel than formal educational achievement. There is scarcely a single program in the Armed Forces for which discrete measures of aptitudes, weak as they may be, are not *much* better predictors of performance than educational achievement.

Methodology is better examined in each of the separate contexts in which specific methodological options were exercised. Our research moved on a broad front in the interest of detecting the direction of the effects of education in juxtaposition with other "variables." The cumulative weight of the evidence, together with the diverse character of the data collected, seems to support the position that we in America ought not to accept education as an unqualified good, without taking account of its negative correlates. Moreover, we must recognize the possibility that the positive effects of increasing educational achievement reported in some analyses, especially those by economists, include a number that have been inferred from somewhat spurious correlations.

II Education in Economic Perspective

Faithful adherence to tribal values requires that a discussion of education begin with the recognition that it is a good thing in itself. Unlike Oscar Wilde's cynic, who knew the price of everything and the value of nothing, Americans are eager to acknowledge the liberating and otherwise personally gratifying effects of time spent in the house of intellect. In PTA manuals, commencement speeches, and college catalogues, zealous defenders of culture and learning express paeans to the "well-rounded man." And few doubt the benefits to a democratic society of a citizenry whose constructive participation in the process of self-government is enhanced by the "decent respect for the opinions of mankind" that can best be learned as part of the educational experience.

These widely held and entrenched beliefs have caused economists to be wary in their studies of expenditures for education, although they have long known that people, or their productive capacities, are an important part of what Adam Smith called the wealth of nations. While a few economists in recent years have sought to pursue the implications of the fact that people "invest" large sums in themselves, others have objected that the mere thought of investment in human beings is offensive. In a discussion of the point, one of the leading economists at work in this field has written:

> Our values and beliefs inhibit us from looking upon human beings as capital goods, except in slavery, and this we abhor. We

are not unaffected by the long struggle to rid society of indentured service and to evolve political and legal institutions to keep men free from bondage. These are achievements that we prize highly. Hence, to treat human beings as wealth that can be augmented by investment runs counter to deeply held values. It seems to reduce man once again to a mere material component, to something akin to property. And for man to look upon himself as a capital good, even if it did not impair his freedom, may seem to debase him.[1]

Accordingly, a colleague, from his position of leadership in an important professional society, has charged that the economics profession is demeaned by analyses which indiscriminately draw analogies between physical capital and the "human capital" that is "formed" by education; the calculation of rates of return on education, he argues, represents a form of misplaced empiricism. For him and others, the most significant benefits of education, including the critical faculties of educated men and women that lead them to change society, are not amenable to quantitative techniques.[2] Faith, at least as much as reason, should guide our worship at the shrine of knowledge.

In their daily living, however, few Americans see any conflict between education as an end in itself and education as a means to other, "lesser" ends. A bizarre expression of this attitude is observable among some of the students who have recently upset university campuses and who have demanded that courses be offered, with academic credit, in methods of campus revolt.

Social scientists presumably pervert education no more

[1] Theodore W. Schultz, "Investment in Human Capital," *American Economic Review*, LI (1961), 1–17, reprinted in Marc Blaug, ed., *Economics of Education*, I (Baltimore: Penguin Books, 1969), p. 14.
[2] Neil Chamberlain, "Second Thoughts on the Concept of Human Capital," Presidential address, Industrial Relations Research Association, 1967, reprinted in *The Development and Use of Manpower: Proceedings of the Twentieth Annual Winter Meeting* (Madison, Wisc.: 1968), pp. 1–13.

than academic purists when they seek to identify the rather large "residual" secular benefits that remain after appropriate expression has been given to education's loftier meanings.[3] One need not contest or even gainsay the highminded view of education held by the critics of the "human capital" school, as Professor Schultz has pointed out. "There is nothing in the concept of human wealth contrary to [J. S. Mill's] idea that [wealth] exists only for the advantage of people; by investing in themselves, people can enlarge the range of choice available to them. It is one way free men can enhance their welfare."[4]

Nor is it helpful to disregard the real world surrounding teachers, classrooms, and students in the service of a narrow, highly principled position on the qualitative significance of education to men in society. The fact is that education costs money; as an object of expenditures, public and personal, it will and must, therefore, be compared with other objects for which scarce resources are to be allocated by individuals and by the nation, since there are both individual and social costs to consider. It is also a fact that the educational credentials of people typically have a determinate effect, not only on the types of opportunities they will have in American society, but on whether they will have any opportunities at all.

These facts and the implications that immediately arise from them make sensitivity to the economics of education mandatory, even at the risk of taking off the emperor's robes. Surely, the most idealistic would take comfort from any evidence that their intentions concerning education are at the very least *consistent* with a modicum of social efficiency and a maximum of social equity.

[3] Whether the system of education in fact produces well-rounded Americans rather than cultural doughnuts is a question we typically leave to professionals in the nation's schools of education. The trained incapacities of some of these investigators may combine with their vested interests to protect us all, purists included, from the risk that any of the arguments concerning the merits of education will be much shaken by skillful and imaginative research.

[4] Schultz, *op. cit.*, p. 14.

The materials considered in this and the following chapter bear upon questions generated by the fact of education's cost and the fact of our legitimate concern with efficiency in America. For it is often implied by policy, when indeed it is not made explicit in the rhetoric of those who justify the *status quo*, that our investments in education are a factor in efficiency; that they are "needed" or "required," speaking in economic terms. It is therefore useful to identify the contributions of education to the commonwealth in socioeconomic as well as in purely cultural and intellectual terms. Does the commonwealth benefit from investments in education as much as, more, or less than the people who are educated? How do social and individual costs differ? Are there technical or, better, "functional" requirements for capabilities linked to formal education in the workaday economy, and, if there are, do they exceed in the aggregate or do they fall below the achievements of the "work force"? What methodological problems lie in the way of answers to questions pertaining to the operation of the market in which the supply and demand for education are alleged to operate?

In a society in which the market is supposed to allocate resources and, in the process, to punish inefficiency, in which full employment is a statutory objective, and in which material wellbeing is often regarded as a prerequisite to a stable and responsive political system, we wonder whether on balance there is reason or prejudice in the short-run decision-making processes that link education to the work opportunities and welfare of citizens. To put this in another way, the market imperfections in the supply and demand of education may be more important for some policy purposes than the actual definition of long-run equilibrium.

Americans who value work, individualism, and material progress often view with equanimity the disadvantages of those who stand outside their system of production. Their assumption that the education-employment nexus is rationally defined—*i.e.*, that the market is operating—squares with the judgment that those without credentials simply do not qualify for jobs and that these wretches have largely themselves to blame for their lot. The same logic can be (and often is) applied in connection with occupational mobility and income among the employed members of the American community as well: if the educational requirements for better jobs are real —that is, "functionally" necessary—and if educational opportunities are available, then the individual knows almost precisely "where it's at."

The Economic Criteria for Education and the Development of "Human Capital"

The economics of education developed relatively recently in response to "the puzzle confronting economists . . . that the rate of growth in the output that was being observed has been much larger than the rate of increase in the principal resources that were being measured."[5] On closer inspection, the "puzzle" turned out to be a problem created by economists themselves; in studies of increases in national product, they had been using such narrowly defined and refined estimates of capital and labor that they had excluded qualitative improvements in both these resources.

The remedy was a number of studies pointing to improvements in the quality of labor as one of the major sources of economic growth. These efforts were in many cases informed by the idea that investments in "human capital" could be treated, with minor modifications in conventional theories of investment, in the same manner as investments in physical capital.

[5] Theodore W. Schultz, "Reflections on Investment in Man," Supplement, Oct., 1962, "Investment in Human Beings," *Journal of Political Economy*, LXX, Part 2 (1962), 3.

Reviews of the statistical association between educational investments and growth rates provided sharp presumptive evidence that the educational achievements of a nation's work force was a significant factor in improving the "quality" of labor as a "factor of production." Two facts, however, alerted economists to the likelihood that such cross-cultural data deserved more careful interpretation. First, as Bowen points out,[6] there was considerable dispersion in the correlations between school-enrollment ratios and GNP per capita among countries, particularly in the middle range. Second, it is clear that there can be problems in countries that educate a stratum of the population whose occupational expectations are well beyond the opportunities the economy may provide in the short or even the long run.

Even allowing that the quality and distribution of investments in education are of greater moment than the quantity alone, education, it is commonly argued, makes three direct and fundamental contributions to economic development.[7] First, new techniques and ideas flow from higher education and research establishments, and these new techniques can be embodied in physical capital, which in turn determines the rate at which an economy can advance. Second, the more rapidly new skills can be given to members of the work force, "the more easily they are able to make use of production techniques, and the more likely they are to initiate changes in methods of production and methods of organization."[8] A

[6] William G. Bowen, "Assessing the Economic Contribution of Education: An Appraisal of Alternative Approaches," in Seymour Harris, ed., *Economic Aspects of Higher Education* (Paris: Organization for Economic Cooperation and Development, 1964), pp. 177–200.

[7] John Vaizey, *Education in the Modern World* (London: World University, 1967), pp. 52–53.

[8] *Ibid.*, p. 53. This process is identified as an outcome of formal education. It is worth noting that there is evidence pointing to the increasing role of schooling over on-the-job training in America. See Jacob Mincer, "On-the-Job Training: Costs, Returns and Some Implications," in "Investment in Human Beings," *Journal of Political Economy*, LXX, Part 2 (1962), 50–73.

third but less tangible aspect of education's role inheres in the "underlying complex of relationships and attitudes which link consumers and workers and management."[9]

These are reasonable statements as they stand, and they will upset few since they assert no specific ideas about magnitudes and weights. Economists, however, like other scientists, are not typically satisfied with broad qualitative statements, and a number of them have attempted to give specificity to their theoretical formulations. Among the most interesting of these attempts are those that seek to identify the personal and social rates of return on investments in education, and those that seek to identify the contribution of education to the portion of economic growth that remains after the contributions of other factors of production have been considered.

Despite differences in the detailed calculations as well as in the scope of these attempts to quantify education as an "economic good," they may for present purposes be considered together.[10] These studies have a number of revealing similarities that are more relevant in the present context than their differences in methodological tactics or over-all strategic purposes.

They measure the nation's formal educational "input" in years of schooling of the employed labor force. Apart from distinguishing in some instances among levels of schooling, they do not usually differentiate education by type or quality —that is, professional *versus* vocational education, or education in prosperous suburban schools compared with that in the schools of poverty-ridden inner-city areas. With a few exceptions, definitions of education used in the most widely cited studies, including those cited in this chapter, tend to

[9] Vaizey, *op. cit.*, p. 53.

[10] Bowen, *op. cit.*; Bruce Wilkinson, *Studies in the Economics of Education* (Ottawa: The Queen's Printer, 1965), Chapter I; Seymour Harris, "General Problems of Education and Manpower," in Harris, ed., *op. cit.*, pp. 11–95; Mary Jean Bowman, "The Human Investment Revolution in Economic Thought," *Sociology of Education*, XXXIX (1966), 111–37; and Schultz, *op. cit.*

homogenize what on even perfunctory inspection is a heterogeneous variable.

Education is often presumed also to be a continuous variable; approximately the same marginal differences in the economic values are assumed to exist between, say, any two successive years of high school. And researchers assume this despite the recurrent finding that diplomas and degrees command a price in the labor market that goes well beyond the marginal increment of learning that may be achieved between the third and fourth year of high school or college.[11] An extreme example: A number of law schools have recently begun awarding a doctorate to their graduates in place of the traditional Bachelor of Laws degree. As a result, these graduates *automatically* start at higher civil-service classifications if they go to work for the federal government, even though their preparation has not changed.

In some studies, on-the-job training is not broken out for separate analysis and so it becomes a tricky matter to draw conclusions about the distinctive role of formal schooling. As one economist has noted, "what schooling contributes [to national product] depends upon the factors with which human skills are combined in production and the opportunities for on-the-job learning and training, which are in turn functions of the pace of change."[12]

The cross-sectional data on age cohorts that are typically used in studies of the economic returns to education pose problems as well, for they present only approximations of lifetime earnings. This fact makes it difficult to draw accurate inferences about the actual "returns" on education, and the results vary a good deal depending on whether average or

[11] Once again there are exceptions; most current research on the economics of education focuses precisely on "the different marginalities at different age levels."

[12] Bowman, *op. cit.*, p. 119. For an estimate of the degree of the dependence to which Professor Bowman refers, see Mincer, *op. cit.*

median income figures are used for the categories of people whose incomes and achievements are compared and analyzed.[13]

The analysis of the costs of education, against which its benefits might be juxtaposed, is also fraught with difficulties, and economists have reached less than full agreement on its clarification.[14] Among the biggest bones of doctrinal contention is the manner in which best to handle the "incomes foregone" by people engaged in study. Those economists who are concerned with the workaday operations of the economy (who therefore have a strongly "institutionalist" orientation) worry about calculations of foregone earnings that assume the employability of school attenders; they argue that such assumptions are suspect in the presence of significant unemployment. Even freewheeling model-builders are a little restive about this issue, although some assume that working-age members of the population who are enrolled in school would earn not only as much as their fully employed, less educated peers but more, because they "are superior in intelligence, ambition, and dependability to those who would have better employment opportunities."[15] The reasoning, meanwhile, that

> . . . the "sudden" appearance of some ten million young people on the labor market could not result in anything but wholesale unemployment . . . would be fallacious since there is no question of actual transfer, either sudden or gradual,

[13] See Harris, op. cit. Professor Gary Becker uses both average and median earnings in his analysis and argues that the former "are clearly more appropriate when calculating cohort gains; perhaps medians are better for other purposes" (Human Capital, New York: Columbia University Press, 1964, p. 76). Average incomes have an upward bias owing to the effect of a relatively small number of very high incomes.

[14] For a helpful and essentially nontechnical discussion, see M. Blaug, "The Rate of Return on Investment in Education," in Blaug, op. cit., pp. 231–36, reprinted from The Manchester School, XXXIII (1965).

[15] Fritz Machlup, The Production and Distribution of Knowledge in the United States (Princeton: Princeton University Press, 1962). p. 95. Professor Machlup does not commend such an assumption; he merely says that this would be "another procedure" regarding opportunity costs in studies of education.

from school to the labor market. The comparison is between hypothetical systems, both long established and well functioning; hence no transition period, no adjusting with frictions, need be taken into account.[16]

"Hypothetical systems," of course, can always be made to be "well functioning." Such a statement by itself, however, provides a wondering critic with no reassurance concerning various estimates of earnings potentials of students-turned-employees. Imperfections in the market for labor make it difficult to accept the "marginalist" argument without reservation or qualification. Nevertheless, estimates of such earnings potentials are used in numerous studies reported in the economics literature when foregone earnings—as much as three fifths of the cost of education in some studies—are added to other educational costs. The argument tends to slip from assumption to policy recommendation rather too quickly in these studies to leave one entirely sanguine about the inadequacy of the logic or the possibility that the dislocation problem to which Professor Machlup refers is merely one of marginal significance and of short- *versus* long-run nature.

There are, after all, many steps on a scale between one "marginal" student who chooses work over study and "ten million" extra young people in the labor market, as an examination of the rewards to workers of different educational achievements makes clear. Thus the large numbers of young people with college-level abilities who do not attend college will not necessarily earn incomes substantially higher than others who enter the work force either after high school or during their high-school years. As Professor Becker points out in a summary at the end of his path-breaking analysis,

General observation indicates that college graduates tend to be more "able" than high-school graduates, apart from the effect

16 *Ibid.*, p. 94.

of college education. This is indicated also by information gathered on I.Q., rank in class, father's education or income, physical health, ability to communicate, and several other distinguishing characteristics. A few studies permit some assessment of the relative importance of ability and education in explaining earning differentials between college and high-school persons. By and large, it appears, ability explains only a relatively small part of the differentials, and college education explains the larger part. Apparently, moreover, the rate of return from college is positively related to the level of ability since there is evidence that *ability plays a larger part in determining the earnings of college than high-school persons.*[17]

It has also been established, in analyses of wage differentials between whites and nonwhites, that the latter will have lower earnings than whites *in each category of educational achievement,* a fact that underscores the considerable difficulties of dealing with the matter of foregone incomes in calculating private returns on educational investment. Indeed, these difficulties highlight the importance of employment levels and such related factors as "market and nonmarket discrimination." The average 1967 income among nonwhite men who had completed high school or had one year of college or more, and who were employed in March, 1968, was about three fourths the average of similarly situated white men.[18] These disparities occur no matter how the data are broken down; Dr. Waldman, an economist in the Bureau of Labor Statistics, points out:

> Even within an occupation group, nonwhite workers are more likely to be found in the less skilled, lower paying jobs. Among men employed as white-collar workers, there was little difference in 1968 in the median years of school completed—13.3 for white men and 13.0 for the nonwhites. Despite this, in every

[17] Becker, *op. cit.,* p. 154-55. Emphasis added.
[18] Elizabeth Waldman, "Educational Attainment of Workers," *Monthly Labor Review,* XCII (February, 1969), 14-22.

educational category, average nonwhite income was $2,000 to $2,500 lower than white income.

Better educated nonwhite men frequently have the same if not lower income as lesser educated white men in the same occupation. In white-collar work, the average income for white men who had completed elementary school or less ($5,900) was about the same as that for nonwhite men who had high school diplomas. In professional, technical, or related jobs, white high school graduates averaged about $8,550 in 1967 compared with $6,200 for nonwhite men with one to three years of college and $8.050 for nonwhite college graduates. White college graduates in professional and related occupations averaged $10,500. The same income relationships held true among blue-collar and service workers.[19]

The cumulative effect of marginal cases on the aggregated data do not, therefore, leave one entirely comfortable with the dichotomy implied in theoretical thinking on the subject of earnings, educational achievement, and employment.

Another issue that attends the marginalist argument has to do with the fact that a useful estimate of foregone earnings must take into account the alternative uses to which educational dollars might be put by the investor. Professor Bowen makes this technical point clearly in a classic survey of the published literature on the economics of education:

Since the monetary benefits of education accrue over time, it is necessary to use some discount factor to take account of the fact that a dollar earned tomorrow is less valuable than a dollar earned today, and computations of the present value of the future stream of benefits to be expected from education are, of course, very sensitive to the discount factor used. Houthakker has made some calculations (based on 1950 census data for the United States) which indicate that the capital value (present value) at age 14 of before-tax lifetime income associated with four or more years of college ranged from a figure of $280,989

[19] *Ibid.*, p. 22.

if a zero discount rate is used to $106,269 at a 3-per-cent rate of discount to $47,546 at 6 per cent and to $30,085 at 8 per cent. Unfortunately, there is no simple answer to the question of what is the right discount factor, and this question has in fact been the subject of considerable debate.[20]

Income as a Measure of the Value of Education

Many of the issues generated in efforts to assess the personal or social costs of education are related to an even more fundamental problem than that of foregone earnings. In nearly all empirical studies of the economics of education, the income of population groups differentiated by education is considered a measure of their productivity—that is to say, of the contribution of each educational group to the economy. The logic involved in such formulations, which human-capital theory borrowed from earlier and more general economic thinking, has gained credibility from its widespread use in the study of education.

The result is that the problematical quality of assumptions linking productivity to income by using education as an "independent variable" is scarcely recognized in economic research that draws on human-capital studies. To cite a recent example, a high positive correlation between rates of change in output per worker and total labor compensation over ten industry groups suggests to the researcher that "differential trends in productivity have been associated with differential trends in labor quality."[21] In a footnote at this point, he adds:

[20] W. G. Bowen, "Assessing the Economic Contribution of Education: An Appraisal of Alternative Approaches," *Higher Education*, report of the Committee under the Chairmanship of Lord Robbins, 1961–63 (London, HMSO, 1963), Appendix IV, pp. 73–96, Comnd 2154-4. Reprinted in Blaug, *op. cit.*, pp. 67–100; citation from p. 90.

[21] Victor R. Fuchs, *The Service Economy* (New York: Columbia University Press, 1968), p. 60. "Labor quality" in this study includes age, sex,

"An alternative inference—that the differential trends in compensation are a result of the weakness of competitive forces and are unrelated to labor quality—seems less plausible but cannot be rejected *a priori*."[22] Here the matter drops from sight; no further attempt is made to explore the suggested alternative.

What makes it "less plausible" is the underlying assumption about the relationship of wages and productivity that informs neoclassical marginal analysis. The objections of economists who do not accept the proposition that earnings are an indicator either of productivity or of educational achievements embodied in productivity are not identical, but they are sufficiently similar to summarize together.

It has been argued that earnings reflect ability more than they do educational achievements, but this question has been clarified somewhat by studies purporting to show that educational achievement is a more powerful predictor of earnings than ability when ability is measured by I.Q. scores and class standing.[23] Such findings raise two different issues. First, they imply that the credentials are more important determinants than naked ability, or at least that the training component of educational experience has a more pronounced effect than general educational development.

Secondly, one might question the adequacy of measures of ability that rest largely on reading skills. The reader may ponder for himself the logic (and equity) of crediting with high intelligence those comfortable sons of the middle- and upper-income groups who have highly developed reading skills, extensive educational exposure, and high income while gain-

---

and color as well as education, but the logic is the same; the example was chosen for its explicitness.

22 *Ibid.*

23 See Edward F. Denison, "Appendix to Edward F. Denison's Reply," in Study Group in the Economics of Education, *The Residual Factor and Economic Growth* (Paris: Organization for Economic Cooperation and Development, 1964), pp. 86–100; and Becker, *op. cit.*, Part II.

saying the intelligence of less fortunate young people whose deplorable school experiences rarely facilitate performance on tests or in classrooms but whose survival gives abundant testimony that they are not fools.

Consider also that in our way of life there are abilities and abilities. It is by no means clear how one can defend a system of income distribution without falling back on a set of values. The economy rewards some abilities well and others not at all. As Paul Samuelson once pointed out, it is singularly easy to account in technical economic terms for the differences in wages between butchers and surgeons; a more complex logic might be needed, however, to explain why plastic surgeons typically earn more than cardiac surgeons.[24]

Perhaps it is sufficient to remind ourselves that a number of complex issues arise in the use of income data. The fact of the matter is that the use of data on earnings involves different problems depending on where one stands; the idea that "we are paid what we are worth" is more easily accepted by those who stand on any given rung when they look *down* than when they look *up* the income ladder. The idea that income reflects productivity leaves open the prior issue of the determinants of productivity, but whether these be ability or surrogates for ability, such as education, certain other problems remain that weaken the causal linkages.

One difficulty arises in the way in which the income of a nation is computed. By definition, the earnings of individuals represent their contribution to national income, which is, after all, simply the sum of individual incomes. The trouble is that there are some people, as everybody, including economists, knows—hard-working wives and mothers, for example—who contribute to social welfare even though they are not in the "labor force."

This omission, however, is not the only source of distortion.

24 Paul Samuelson, *Economics: An Introductory Analysis*, 6th ed. (New York: McGraw Hill, 1964), p. 560.

The analysis of the contribution of education (or human capital, more broadly defined) to productivity and economic growth rests on the neoclassical concept of the production function, a (mathematical) function showing for a given state of technological knowledge the greatest output quantities that can be obtained from any quantitative combination of various input factors.[25] Of this method, Erik Lundberg has remarked:

> If the total income distribution from period to period is determined mainly, or at least substantially, by factors other than marginal productivity relations, then we cannot be so sure that an estimate of the relative contribution coming from the input-factors can be based on national income shares.[26]

When Lundberg points to "factors other than marginal productivity relations," he is implying that market imperfections may have more to do with income distribution than the maximizing behavior attributed to a firm under perfect competition. When economists cross their marginal cost and revenue curves, they are, of course, thinking about hypothetical firms. They do not allow for such distortions as employers with the market power to indulge their tastes; the tendency to create a corps of permanent workers in internal labor markets; the typically limited information of job-seekers; and

[25] Evidence that academics, including economists, do not fetter themselves with the detailed trappings of production functions may be found in the pages of the *Bulletin of the American Association of University Professors*, in which economists examine university pay scales. Most professors would have to acknowledge their gratitude to Professor Baumol for his imaginative efforts in his colleagues' behalf; some of them may even be glad that he foregoes a discussion of academics' productivity in these helpful and scholarly presentations.

[26] Erik Lundberg, "Comments on Mr. Edward F. Denison's Paper," in Study Group in the Economics of Education, *op. cit.*, p. 69. In this same context, Professor Lundberg points out (p. 68) that "the great explanatory importance that Denison can attribute to education, in fact, depends on the big share of labor income, 70–75 per cent. The low share of capital, 20–25 per cent, gives this factor its subordinate position and instead permits more room for the residual."

the growing importance of noncompetitive groups of workers where the distinctions among groups are not necessarily continuous increments of skill or education but roles, socially defined on the basis of such variables as age, sex, and color. Furthermore, when they talk about production functions, they are typically talking about long-run trends. The problem begins when we try to fit the experience of real people and real firms into econometric models; as Lord Keynes once reminded us, the economist's long run may be a man's whole lifetime.

In a strong statement on this matter, Lord Balogh argues that the attribution of sensational effects to education is based on calculations in which the larger social framework is utterly disregarded. Instead, human-capital studies

. . . derive a residue of growth rate—i.e., that part of the growth rate which, on the basis of their own particular assumptions and constructions, remains unexplained by the increase of other factors of production—a conclusion unproven and unprovable. They then assume, equally unwarrantably, that investment in education is not merely a cause (rather than the effect, or one of several conditions) but the sole and sufficient cause responsible for the whole, or a certain artificially selected portion, of this residual growth experienced in certain historical examples.[27]

They then reverse the roles of the historical conditions and the so-called input factors and make an "iron law of education."[28]

Although Lord Balogh imputes a stronger position to the marginalists and growth economists than they themselves claim—certainly they have formulated no "iron laws"—he nevertheless reminds us that the results of many economic studies of education are at least in significant degree an arti-

---

[27] Thomas Balogh, "Comments on the Paper of Messrs. Tinbergen and Bos," in *Study Group in the Economics of Education, op. cit.*, p. 183.
[28] *Ibid.*

fact of the assumptions that inform the work, including the "marginalist" assumptions concerning the relationship between wages and productivity.

Without passing judgment on the matters in dispute, we can state that, used with care, the results obtained in the studies referred to have heuristic value.[29] The problems in them, however, inevitably leave us uneasy about their usefulness in helping to establish the *economic* "rationality" of making further gigantic investments in education.

One may be satisfied in the abstract that the classical models are adequate for "understanding," but they clearly do not apply in much detail to the world we know, the world in which policy is made by employers, elected leaders, and others who administer and control the nation's resources. The reader, meanwhile, will find interminable and inconclusive discussions of these issues in the literature of economics, which will convince him that many of the contentious issues in regard to the meaning of wage rates and wage levels must ultimately be regarded as matters of faith.[30]

[29] For a straightforward and lucid discussion of the programmatic utilities of these approaches, see Wilkinson, *op. cit.*, Chapter I. The ultimate utility of these approaches will be a function, not only of the resolution of the issues discussed here, but of other issues that bear, particularly, on the social gains of education to society. This question is only opened up in the present discussion.

[30] For an empirical analysis of wage rates and wage levels, see Richard Lester and Joseph Shister, eds., *Insights into Labor Issues* (New York: Macmillan, 1948), pp. 197ff. See also John T. Dunlop, "The Task of Contemporary Wage Theory," in George W. Taylor and Frank C. Pierson, eds., *New Concepts of Wage Determination* (New York: McGraw-Hill, 1957), pp. 117–39; E. Robert Livernash, "The Internal Wage Structure," in Taylor and Pierson, eds., *op. cit.*, pp. 140–72. For theoretical discussions, see Fritz Machlup, "Theories of the Firm: Marginalist, Behavioral, Managerial." *American Economic Review*, LVII (1967), 1–33: and Dennis H. Robertson, "Wage Grumbles," in William Fellner and Bernard F. Haley, eds., *Readings in the Theory of Income Distribution* (London: Allen and Unwin, 1954), pp. 221–36.

It should be emphasized, as Barbara Wootton remarked in a related context, that

> Nothing that has been said must be construed as evidence that classical wage theory, within the limits of its own carefully defined assumptions, is actually wrong. Indeed, it is characteristic of this and other economic theories that they are cast in a shape in which it is impossible to prove them wrong.[31]

Our confidence in the economic criteria that might be used to help us make sense out of the implications of policy options would be enhanced if we could fall back on more direct methods of establishing the needs, narrowly speaking, for education in our complex economy than may be inferred from studies based on classical wage theory. The idea that rate-of-return analysis provided an insufficient basis for educational policy decisions was the impetus for a more direct type of research carried out by R. S. Eckaus in 1964[32] and subsequently by several others. Despite innumerable methodological difficulties, their procedures, with some revisions and appropriate updating, facilitate a discussion of the changing relationship between job "requirements" and the educational achievements of the working population. The next chapter presents the results of an extension of this earlier work.

[31] Barbara Wootton, *The Social Foundations of Wage Policy* (New York: Norton, 1955), p. 67.
[32] R. S. Eckaus. "Economic Criteria for Education and Training," *Review of Economics and Statistics*, XLIV (1964), 181–90.

III Job Requirements and Educational Achievement

Professor R. S. Eckaus, of the Massachusetts Institute of Technology, is one economist who has misgivings about the "human capital" approach to education when the term "capital" is used almost precisely as in analyses of physical capital. To him the term is permissible only when it is used in a loose way, to denote an idea, an analogy, without any implication that educated people should be handled as physical capital—in the national accounts, for example. He argues that prices, while useful in making estimates that may serve as a basis for policy decisions on the allocation of resources, "must reflect the relative scarcities of the factors involved."[1]

He argues, further, that wages and salaries are not "reasonably good prices in the markets for education and educated labor which can be used for valuing 'human capital' and its return," and he goes on to discuss market imperfections, the difficulties in identifying the benefits of education to the firm or the worker, and other problems in accounting and in estimating relevant dimensions of the supply of and demand for education and educated people.[2] "The existence of real economic requirements for education and training," he maintains, "is not contradicted by the presence of various obstacles to the use of market values in measuring the amount of productive

[1] R. S. Eckaus, "Economic Criteria for Education and Training," *Review of Economics and Statistics*, XLVI (1964), 181–90.
[2] *Ibid.*, p. 182.

38

education and the return on it. An alternative approach is to attempt to estimate these requirements directly."[3]

The approach in which the demand for particular categories of "educated" labor is compared with supply, as Eckaus has pointed out, is not a novel one. Professor Seymour Harris, in an earlier and more controversial study, used a less detailed set of calculations than those reported in the following pages or those presented by Eckaus. Professor Harris advised in 1949 that parents, policy makers, and students be mindful that America was producing more college graduates than could be absorbed into occupations they would "expect" to fill and at the relatively high salaries such occupations traditionally have commanded; his suggestion receives some support in the present study.[4]

The term "some support" is used advisedly, for the data are subject to manipulation in accordance with several sets of assumptions about the meaning of various levels of educational requirements for jobs, and about the relevance to actual behavior on the job of formal educational achievements that exceed the minimum functional requirements for adequate job performance.[5] On the last point, our efforts both help and

---

[3] *Ibid.*, p. 183.

[4] See Seymour Harris, *The Market for College Graduates* (Cambridge: Harvard University Press, 1949, p. 64. I gratefully acknowledge the collaboration of Marcia K. Freedman, of the Columbia University Conservation of Human Resources Project, in the preparation of this and the early sections of the following chapter. The job was an extensive and detailed one and was successfully completed only because she willingly bore its considerable burdens and because she has the necessary technical skills and imagination. We discovered together that, as Professor Parnes pointed out in a review of the manpower-forecasting approach, "despite the limitations, the approach [of Eckaus] is deserving of additional experimentation. However, the basic data required for the analysis would take considerable time to develop." See his "Relation of Occupation to Educational Qualification," reprinted in M. Blaug, ed. *Economics of Education, I* (Baltimore: Penguin Books, 1968), p. 284. We were assisted in the task by Gretchen Maclachlan, whose skills were gratefully exploited, and by Hugh Appet.

hinder us in attempting to clarify the degree to which educational achievements of people in an occupational category are the result of sensible employers' efforts to improve the "quality" of their work forces when loose labor markets permit them to raise educational requirements, or are simply a reflection of the "taste" (or prejudices) of employers.[6]

On the one hand, because the data are longitudinal in nature, our efforts help make it possible, with a few parsimonious assumptions, to discover whether job requirements are changing faster than the population's educational achievements or *vice versa*. On the other hand, they hinder clarification because they make no allowance for the contribution of "excess" education to employers and their firms, a matter considered in later chapters. The issue is a crucial one and requires that we go beyond standard economic approaches, both direct and indirect, in order to speculate intelligently about whether the "excess" education is a boon, a bane, or a matter of no moment to employers and their workers.

Job Requirements and Occupational Scales

Earlier research points strongly to the proposition that, with the exception of "professionals and ditchdiggers," with respect to single personal traits and characteristics, occupations

---

which are fulfilled by formal education. To the extent that employers screen applicants according to educational achievements, we may use the term "requirements" rather broadly.

[6] In this regard, both Professors M. W. Reder and Albert Rees, in their respective reviews of Gary Becker's work (cited earlier), suggest, for example, that the earnings advantages of college graduates are less a reflection of the greater productivity of better-educated workers than of the prejudices of employers. See M. W. Reder, "Gary Becker's *Human Capital: A Review Article,*" *Journal of Human Resources,* II (Winter 1967), 103; and A. Rees (Book Review), *American Economic Review,* LV (1965), 950–60.

cannot be placed in a hierarchical order that corresponds to the income hierarchy of occupations; variations in the characteristics of people performing adequately *within* occupational groups have been found to be as great as variations *among* these groups.[7]

The review by Lawrence G. Thomas, the study by Thorndike, and the technical discussion of personnel-selection devices cited here all make it clear that job requirements must be conceived as complex *patterns* rather than in unidimensional terms. In the first two references, data on the civilian occupations and personal attributes of large samples of American military personnel during both world wars provide strong circumstantial evidence that Americans of diverse educational achievements perform productive functions adequately and perhaps well in all but a few professional occupations.

These studies also make it clear that it is not possible to construct an occupational scale according to the intellectual abilities required by diverse occupations. To be sure, some correspondence between job levels and test scores was revealed in a study of the Army General Classification Test scores of more than 81,000 men in 227 occupations. On the face of it, such test data would be encouraging if the prospect of a national scale of occupational differences depended only on the validity of the sample and the reliability of the measures used. The difficulty that plagues this approach, however, as Professor Thomas points out, is that there is

. . . striking *variation* in test scores made by members of any *one* occupation . . . . If we examine the variation in test scores

[7] Lawrence G. Thomas, *The Occupational Structure and Education* (Englewood Cliffs: Prentice-Hall, 1956); Robert L. Thorndike, "The Prediction of Vocational Success," in John T. Flynn and Herbert Garber, eds., *Assessing Behavior: Readings in Educational and Psychological Measurement* (Reading, Mass.: Addison-Wesley, 1967), pp. 240–55; and Marvin D. Dunnette, *Personnel Selection and Placement* (Belmont, Calif.: Wadsworth, 1966).

in only those 172 occupations from which at least fifty enlisted men were drawn (so that our samples will be large enough to show characteristic distributions), we find that men scoring 108.3 points [the mean, or average, of the median scores of all 227 occupations] would rank above the lowest quartile of *all but 26* of these 172 occupations, and would rank above the lowest 10 per cent in all but nine occupations.[8]

Such data obviously discourage us from translating occupational wage differences into ability differences and encourage us to find alternative ways of characterizing job requirements.

Professor Thomas himself commended the job classifications that were being developed by the United States Employment Service's Occupational Analysis Section at the time he conducted his examination of education and occupational structure. The classifications that resulted from the agency's efforts are those used by Eckaus, to whose work reference has been made, and by other investigators whose methods and results are related to the present use of these classifications.[9] These studies employed estimates of "general educational development" (GED) required for jobs, estimates that were constructed through the collaboration of personnel from the Division of Placement Methods, the Occupational Analysis Branch, and the Entry Occupations Sections, all of the Bureau of Employment Security (BES) of the United States Employment Service.

[8] Thomas, *op. cit.*, p. 265. The categories and classification systems used would not adequately account for these results. Emphasis in the original.

[9] The first of these anticipated the others; it used categories approximating those of the 1940 and 1950 censuses and was based upon the *minimum* amount of education demanded by employers of job applicants in 2,216 occupations in 18 industries. See H. M. Bell, *Matching Youth and Jobs* (Washington: American Council on Education, 1940). The others: Bruce Wilkinson, "Some Aspects of Education in Canada," unpublished doctoral dissertation, MIT, 1964; John G. Scoville, "Education and Training Requirements for Occupations," *Review of Economics and Statistics*, XLVIII (1966), 387–94.

Confidence in these estimates of education (and training)[10] requirements for jobs is obviously contingent upon the validity of the scale of GED requirements that was constructed from job descriptions. Since the findings of the studies, including this one, depend so heavily on the scale of GED requirements, it is appropriate to describe that scale here. A lengthy description of the procedure involved in making the estimates in the first (1956) analysis of jobs is available elsewhere.[11]

The GED scale embraces three types of development—reasoning, mathematical, and language. Each of these was estimated separately on a scale from 1 (low) to 7 (high), and the final estimate of the requirement of each job in the analysis was the highest of the three. For this reason, and also because of variation in the quality of schooling and the possibility of learning from other experience, the Bureau specifically eschewed any attempt to translate GED into levels of educational achievement.[12] Nevertheless, in previous studies, the

[10] The two sets of estimates, one in 1956 and the other in 1966, include estimates of required "specific vocational preparation" (SVP) as well as GED; these training requirements are not considered here.

[11] *Estimates of Worker Trait Requirements for 4,000 Jobs as Defined in the Dictionary of Occupational Titles*, Washington, D.C.: Bureau of Employment Security, U.S. Employment Service, U.S. Department of Labor, 1956, pp. iv–ix, and Appendix A, "Manual for Rating Training Time," pp. 111–20.

[12] "Ordinarily such education is obtained in elementary school, high school, or college. It also derives from experience and individual study." U.S. Department of Labor, Bureau of Employment Security, *Dictionary of Occupational Titles*, 3rd ed. (Washington: Government Printing Office, 1966), Vol. II, p. 651. In the 4,000-trait study already cited, the Bureau stated that "approximate school grade equivalents are provided on the inside of the covers of this volume as an aid in evaluating an applicant's General Educational Development." This passage was deleted, however, by an erratum notation in 1958 ("Correction List No. 1"), and, in fact, no such equivalents were ever placed inside the covers of the volume. The issue is an important one, as Dr. Sidney Fine, who was Chief of the Entry Occupations Section, has emphasized in a review of the weaknesses of studies based upon these trait estimates. See his "The Use of the *Dictionary of Occupational Titles* as a Source of Estimates of Educational and Training Requirements," *Journal of Human Resources*, III (1968), 363–75.

first step was to translate GED into "years of schooling," as follows:

GED	Years of Schooling
1	0
2	4
3	7
4	10
5	12
6	16
7	18

Requirements were then reported as years of schooling, and interpretations made accordingly.

The operational problem for the present research was to compare, through a series of gross estimates, the achieved education of the labor force with the educational requirements of the jobs held for the two census years, 1950 and 1960. Since only the 1956 Worker Traits Analysis was available to previous researchers, they perforce applied the same estimates of requirements to the occupational distributions of the different census years. The publication of the second Worker Traits Analysis in 1966[13] made it possible to include the effects of changes in estimated requirements as well as in the distribution of people among jobs.

To measure the changes in requirements, it was necessary to deal with the same sample of jobs. For this purpose, the 4,000 jobs included in the first analysis were extracted from the 14,000 of the second analysis.[14] Our findings are reported in

---

[13] *Dictionary of Occupational Titles*, 3rd Ed., *op. cit.*, Supplement, *Selected Characteristics of Occupations*.

[14] The task was complicated by the fact that the jobs in the first analysis were designated by the code used in the Second Edition of the *Dictionary of Occupational Titles* (DOT), while the second analysis used the altogether revised coding system of the Third Edition. It was possible, however, to make the translation by using the *Conversion Table of Code and Title Changes Between Second and Third Edition Dictionary of Occupational Titles*. This matching involved many operations, the details of which need

the terms of the second analysis, since we adjusted the seven-point GED scale of the first trait analysis to the second analysis, in which a six-point GED scale was used.

Our second major operation was to assign a GED level to each of 256 occupational groups in the census tables showing years of school completed by the experienced civilian labor force.[15] This was facilitated by work sheets prepared by the Bureau of Employment Security as a first approximation to converting DOT titles to census categories. Once this process was completed, the median GED for each group was weighted by the number of workers. The result was a distribution of educational requirements (GED) for all jobs. Finally, for purposes of comparison, the educational achievements (years of school) of the labor force were reproduced from the same census tables.

Factors Contributing to Changes in Requirements from 1950 to 1960

Table III-1 presents our basic findings—the distribution of the reported educational achievements of the labor force and our estimate (using the method described above) of the distribution of educational requirements for the jobs held by the

---

not detain us here. We are indebted to Frank Cassell, Leon Lewis, Jack Newman, Adeline Padgett, and many others at the U.S. Employment Service for their assistance in this enterprise. They provided cards containing the data from the two "trait" studies, and they gave abundantly of their time and expert advice. We hope we have come close to living within the guidelines they delineated for using the estimates. We are especially grateful to Mr. Lewis and Mr. Newman, who were nearly collaborators with us in our effort. They are, however, in no way responsible for the results and are, in particular, not responsible for the translations we have made.

[15] 1950 Census, *Occupational Characteristics* (Special Report P-E No. 1B), Table 10; 1960 Census, *Occupational Characteristics* (Subject Report PC(2) 7A), Table 9. The 256 groups represent some aggregation, but they cover the entire experienced civilian labor force.

Table III-1

Education and the Experienced Civilian Labor Force, by Sex, 1950 and 1960

	Education Achieved (in millions)			Education Required (Median GED) for Census Occupations (in millions)			Median GED
	Males	Females	Total	Males	Females	Total	
1950							
Less than 8 years	10.3	2.6	12.9	3.8	0.2	3.9	1
8 years	8.1	2.3	10.4	8.9	6.2	15.1	2
1–3 years high school	7.9	3.1	11.0	8.9	6.0	14.9	3
High-school graduate	8.4	4.9	13.3	15.7	1.9	17.7	4
1–3 years college	2.9	1.6	4.5	2.2	1.3	3.5	5
College graduate	2.8	1.2	4.1	0.9	0.2	1.1	6
1960							
Less than 8 years	7.9	2.5	10.4	—	—	—	1
8 years	6.9	2.6	9.5	6.8	2.0	8.8	2
1–3 years high school	9.7	4.7	14.4	14.8	10.6	15.4	3
High-school graduate	10.6	7.1	17.7	12.7	4.9	17.6	4
1–3 years college	4.2	2.4	6.5	8.0	3.3	11.3	5
College graduate	4.3	1.7	6.0	1.2	0.2	1.4	6

labor force. These data are considered in the analysis that follows, first in the disaggregated form of Table III-1, and subsequently in different juxtaposition. Before discussing the relationships between achievements and requirements, however, we must distinguish the factors that produced changes from 1950 to 1960 *within* these distributions.

On the achievement side, the answer is straightforward; the difference simply shows the increase in years of schooling undertaken by the larger labor force. On the requirements side, however, the change in the distributions from 1950 to 1960 is the result of two distinct factors in addition to population growth: (1) the reclassification of the GED required for the component jobs (an artifact of the BES method), and (2) the growth or decline in the numbers of people holding jobs at each level.[16] Of these sources of change, the shifts that are due to reclassification (the "upgrading" or "downgrading") of individual jobs are by far the more important component.

A comparison of the 1956 and 1966 Worker Traits Analyses shows that 54 per cent of the 4,000 jobs retained the same GED, but 31 per cent were rated higher and 15 per cent lower. The majority of shifts were among low-rated jobs, and this may suggest some of the reasons for the general upward trend. Jobs at the lower GED levels tend to be designated by many different titles and vary according to industry and even from firm to firm. Apparently in an effort to simply nomenclature, the BES, in preparing the Third Edition of the *Dictionary of Occupational Titles*, combined a number of titles in the Second Edition into a new single title. The effect of these consolidations on our own study was to reduce the 4,000 job titles in the first Worker Trait Analysis by approximately one third. It was reasonable to expect some consequent up-

[16] Whatever bias stems from our method of aggregation and the choice of medians to represent the occupational groups is consistent for the two census years.

TABLE III-2

PERCENTAGE CHANGE IN EDUCATION REQUIRED
FOR CENSUS OCCUPATIONS, 1950–60

Type of Change in GED for Aggregated Census Occupations, 1950–60	1950 Education Required (Median GED)					
	1	2	3	4	5	6
	Males					
Reclassification of GED	−100	−30	62	−19	182	−5
Population change	0	7	4	0	78	33
Total change	−100	−23	66	−19	260	28
	Females					
Reclassification of GED	−100	−79	35	100	82	−17
Population change	0	11	43	53	69	13
Total change	−100	−68	78	153	151	−4

ward bias, since the GED for the new title had to be high enough to encompass the highest of the old titles. It is possible that this consolidation reflects actual upgrading of a number of low-level jobs. We can speculate that employers, having access to better-educated workers, have in fact expanded the scope of some jobs.

Whatever the reasons for the higher GED requirements, these changes had far more weight than changes in the number of individuals at each level. Table III-2 compares these two types of change for males and females. The total for each column shows the percentage change from 1950 to 1960. Thus, the net decline in jobs for males requiring GED 2 from 1950 to 1960 was 23 per cent.[17]

---

[17] The reader can check this by the following calculation, which uses the appropriate data in Table III-1:

$$\frac{(\text{GED-2 males, 1950}) - (\text{GED-2 males, 1960})}{(\text{GED-2 males, 1950})} = \frac{8.9 - 6.8}{8.9} = 23\%$$

The components of this change were a decrease of 30 per cent in jobs *formerly* classified at this level (weighted by the populations of these groups) and the combined increases of (a) groups reclassified *into* this level and (b) groups that remained the same (7 per cent).

Inspection of each GED level for males and females separately shows only two cases in which the increase in number outweighs the effect of GED reclassification: in jobs for women requiring GED 3, and in jobs for men requiring GED 6. In all the rest, the general upward movement of GED requirements accounts for most of the difference.

Assuming that the requirements presented in Table III-1 represent the best available estimates, while somewhat exaggerating the differences between 1950 and 1960, we can now assess them in light of the achieved education of the experienced civilian labor force. The data in Table III-1 are presented in as many categories as the constraints of the census education classifications allow; nevertheless, a comparison of "required" with achieved education involves equating years of school with specific GED levels. In addition to the problems mentioned earlier in connection with the GED scale itself, there are other difficulties in making this kind of translation; for example, we must assume that education is a continuum measured in "years of school."

Even in the unaggregated data in Table III-1, there are problems of overlapping. It is difficult, for example, to distinguish between the conceptual skills of an eighth-grade graduate and those of a high-school dropout. A more serious problem arises at the upper levels of GED and achieved education. Since the 1950 census did not distinguish those with advanced degrees from other college graduates, our first approximation of a match for jobs requiring GED 6 had to lump *all* college graduates together. This left only college dropouts and two-year technical-school graduates to fill GED 5, in spite of the fact that this is a mixed group including the second-level professions (*e.g.*, musicians, airplane pilots, nurses). In making *any* kind of match, GED 5 is the most difficult; the findings are quite different depending on how this particular problem is solved.

TABLE III-3

FIVE VERSIONS OF THE MATCH BETWEEN EDUCATION ACHIEVED AND EDUCATION REQUIRED (MEDIAN GED): PERCENTAGE DIFFERENCES FOR THE EXPERIENCED CIVILIAN LABOR FORCE, BY SEX, 1950 AND 1960[a]

| Education Match | | % Difference Between Achieved and Required Education | | | | | |
| | | 1950 | | | 1960 | | |
Achieved	Required	Males	Females	Total	Males	Females	Total
Version 1							
Less than 8 years	1	16.1	15.7	15.9	18.1	12.0	16.1
8 years	2	−2.0	−24.6	−8.2	0.2	3.0	1.1
1–3 years high school	3	−2.5	−18.2	−6.9	−11.8	−28.1	−17.1
High-school graduate	4	−18.0	18.9	−7.6	−4.9	10.3	0.1
1–3 years college	5	1.7	1.5	1.6	−8.7	−4.5	−7.4
College graduate	6	4.7	6.7	5.2	7.1	7.3	7.2
Version 2							
Less than high-school graduation	1–2	33.7	10.7	27.3	40.5	37.4	39.5
High-school graduate, some college	3–4	−32.9	−9.0	−26.2	−29.3	−29.0	−29.2
College graduate	5–6	−0.8	−1.7	−1.1	−11.2	−8.4	−10.3
Version 3							
Less than high-school graduation	1–3	11.6	−27.1	0.8	6.5	−13.1	0.1
High-school graduate, some college	4–5	−16.3	20.4	−6.0	−13.6	5.8	−7.3
College graduate	6	4.7	6.7	5.2	7.1	7.3	7.2
Version 4							
Less than high-school graduation	1–3	11.6	−27.1	0.8	6.5	−13.1	0.1
High-school graduate	4	−18.0	18.9	−7.6	−4.9	10.3	0.1
Some college	5–6	6.4	8.2	6.8	−1.6	2.8	−0.2
Version 5							
Less than high-school graduation	1–3	11.6	−27.1	0.8	6.5	−13.1	0.1
High-school graduate, some college	4, 5 —[b]	−13.1	27.4	−1.7	−9.0	13.3	−1.7
College graduate	5+, 6[b]	1.5	−0.3	0.9	2.5	−0.2	1.6

[a] This table was constructed by calculating the per cents for the columns in Table III-1, aggregating the appropriate cells, and subtracting the required education from that achieved.

[b] Occupational groups requiring GED level 5 were divided into those with median educational achievement of less

Comparing Requirements and Achievements

Although there is a finite number of ways in which the data can be arranged, nothing is fixed about the relationship of GED and years of schooling. Depending on different assumptions about their correspondence, that is, about the matching of "requirements" with "achievements," the "direct approach" to the economic criteria for education afforded by this method can yield extraordinarily diverse findings. Thus, for example, whether there is a shortage or an "excess" of college graduates depends on whether jobs requiring a GED of 5 are regarded as jobs for college graduates or as jobs that can be performed adequately by persons who have graduated from high school and have undergone some college training. The rest of this chapter is devoted to a discussion of five different versions of the data which illustrate the importance of the assumptions that inform this kind of research.

Table III-3 presents these versions. For each version, the "required" education for a given group of occupations was subtracted from the achieved education of given labor-force groups. These differences are discussed in the text.

Version 1

Version 1 (Table III-3) shows the percentage differences for the numerical data presented in Table III-1. It exhibits the following features:

1. The excess of individuals with less than an eighth-grade education over the number required for GED-1 jobs was about the same in 1960 as in 1950—about 16 per cent.

2. A comparison of eighth-grade graduates with those in jobs requiring GED 2 shows that the match improved from

1950 to 1960 because the number of these jobs decreased faster than the population of eighth-grade graduates decreased.

3. For GED 3, the match is reversed; the increase in these jobs was greater than the increase in the number of high-school dropouts presumably available to fill these jobs.

4. A comparison of jobs requiring GED 4 (the largest single category of jobs) with high-school graduates (the largest category on the achievement side) shows that the match improved from 1950 to 1960. The proportion of jobs declined and the number of high-school graduates increased; they matched almost perfectly.

5. The increase of jobs at GED level 5 converted an "oversupply" of achievers in this category (individuals with some college) in 1950 to a shortage in 1960.

6. For GED-6 jobs, the "oversupply" of college graduates was even more striking in 1960 than in 1950 (7 per cent compared to 5 per cent).

Version 2

In the second version, the first three achieved-education categories are grouped (non-high-school graduates) and compared with levels 1 and 2 of required education; the high-school graduates and those with some college are compared with levels 3 and 4; finally, the college-graduate group is aligned with levels 5 and 6. Matched in this way, the data support the conclusion that the demand for better-educated workers has far outrun the available supply, a position often taken in connection with policy proposals calculated to upgrade the labor force's educational achievements. Accordingly, there seems to be an enormous and growing shortage of both high-school and college graduates. Such a conclusion draws some support from their wage changes relative to those of the "lowest" educational achievers. Again, however, these wage changes may reflect the tastes, perhaps the prejudices, of employers and must be interpreted with caution.

The assumptions underlying such a construction of the basic data are extreme indeed; one premise would be that high school dropouts can fill only menial jobs. Furthermore, jobs in GED level 3 would have to be defined as requiring high school graduates. Finally, by this logic, jobs at GED levels 5 and 6 can be filled suitably only by college graduates. In this version, in short, all educational requirements are defined at a maximum, and the result approaches the selection practices of employers in periods in which labor markets are "loose."

To accept this set of definitions is to accept the apocalyptic conclusions of some in America who foresee employment in the future only for the highly educated. The fact is, however, that the vast majority of the workers represented in these data *are* employed, and if the match between the job requirements and the achievements were as poor as Version 2 suggests, one could only marvel at the continued progress of the economy and the society it supports. Some readers simply will not find it credible that *two thirds* of the jobs in the American economy required a high school diploma, or more, in 1950; it would be even more incredible if the equivalent requirements covered fully *86 per cent* of the jobs in the '60's.[18]

---

[18] Eli Ginzberg and Neil Chamberlain have cautioned us to temper these words on the grounds that we can too easily consider only one side of the picture. Another colleague reminds us that we imply an excessively narrow conception of a job, and that more realistically we should recognize that if opportunity costs in terms of creativity are included, the "excess" education pays considerable returns. The economy, they argue, might function at even *higher* levels of performance if greater numbers in the work force were well educated, an issue touched on below and in later chapters. The questions they raise go to the heart of the present study and relate to the problem of determining how much more than minimun educational achievements the economy's jobs can absorb. One may at least be suspicious of the proposition that most jobs make much room for the inputs of workers that go beyond task performance, given the foreseeable trends in the managerial arts.

Version 3

In Version 3 most of the assumptions of the previous version are "stood on their head." Here, workers without high-school diplomas are assumed to be capable of filling jobs at GED levels 1, 2, and 3. Grouped in this way, the changes in both requirements and achievements from 1950 and 1960 wash out, leaving a good match at the lower levels of the occupational distribution. High school graduates and those with post-high-school education short of a college degree are matched against jobs at GED levels 4 and 5 combined, and college graduates against level 6 jobs. For both 1950 and 1960, the "surplus" of college graduates presumably filled jobs at levels 4 and 5.

The totals, however, obscure important differences between the utilization of men and women. For men, the "oversupply" of achievers at both the top and the bottom level presumably filled the gap at the middle level. The shift of low achievers to middle-level jobs, we hypothesized, is largely attributable to age; that is, older workers with low educational achievements can offer experience as a substitute. Furthermore, long-time incumbents of certain positions often pick up additional skills on the job that permit them to function effectively in organizational slots for which the actual requirements may go up.

Some evidence for this conclusion was obtained by analyzing the educational achievements of workers holding jobs at GED levels 4, 5, and 6.[19] At each of these levels, workers over 45 years of age were underrepresented among college graduates and overrepresented among those with less than a high-school education. For the population in GED 5, for example,

[19] This analysis was limited by the number of discrete groups for which both a median GED and a cross-tabulation from Census that includes age and education were available. The population for which such information was available represented 63 per cent of workers in groups with a GED median of 4, 54 per cent of the GED 5's, and 81 per cent of the GED 6's.

workers over 45 constituted somewhat less than half of the total but 65 per cent of the non-high-school graduates and 36 per cent of the college graduates.

Among women, the disparity between achievements and "requirements" was considerably reduced from 1950 to 1960, but the picture continued to show a general downward trend with considerable "underemployment," since the number of low-level jobs for women continued to exceed the supply of poorly educated women. The higher participation rates of better-educated women undoubtedly account for the disparity between achievements and "requirements" among women; these high rates conspire to reduce the number of lower-level jobs available for less educated women.

Viewing the data in this way points up one of the reasons that unemployment rates are highest for young female Negro high-school dropouts—they are competing unsuccessfully for lower-level jobs with an available, much better-educated population group. The fact that women, for a number of reasons, move in and out of the work force, meanwhile, probably limits their opportunities to obtain higher-level jobs that employers seek to fill with more regular workers.

In this version, as in the unaggregated data in Table III-1, GED level 6 is treated as a separate category consisting of the traditional professions, scientists, and academicians. According to this version, the increase in the proportion of the total labor force in these occupations between 1950 and 1960 was negligible, from 2.0 to 2.1 per cent. Meanwhile, the proportion of college graduates went up 30 per cent, leaving a theoretical "oversupply" of highly educated manpower.

Version 4

From 1950 to 1960, there was a marked increase in the proportion of jobs at GED level 5. It is reasonable to suppose that most of the "surplus" college graduates in Version 3 were in fact employed at level 5. It is therefore worthwhile to see how the match is affected if level-4 jobs are allocated to high-school graduates and levels 5 and 6 are combined and matched with the entire group of those who went to college, whether or not they received a degree. The results appear in Version 4, and here the changes from 1950 to 1960 seem to have brought supply and demand into perfect balance, at least with regard to the totals. This version lends enormous support to recent educational policy, since the increase in achievements in the decade (added to earlier increments) was sufficient to provide the personnel for the vast increase in level-5 jobs.

What would seem to be a highly desirable state of affairs is on closer inspection a somewhat problematical one. While men, according to this version, appear to be increasingly less underutilized,[20] women appear to be *more* underutilized than before.

An even more fundamental objection may be made to the assumption necessary in this version that all GED-5 jobs require college graduates. This large and growing category, as we noted earlier, is a mixture of lower-level professions and white-collar occupations that may be homogeneous with respect to the standards that inhere in the GED apparatus but that vary greatly in certification requirements. Although not all practicing engineers and teachers are college graduates, the trend is to require a baccalaureate degree for new entrants to these occupations. College graduates in these two fields who hold degrees appear in the statistics as having attended college for four or more years. Given their typical academic preparation, however, it might be argued that their time in academe has been spent largely in what the United States Employment

---

[20] Students of American social structure may see in this view of developments a factor of some significance; males with educational achievements that surpass those "required" for the jobs they hold, from one point of view, have been "upwardly mobile."

Service analysts call Specific Vocational Preparation (SVP) and that they have undertaken training rather than education.

Version 5

To avoid such tendentiousness we accepted the conventional definitions and sorted the GED 5's into two groups: those occupations that usually require a four-year college degree of any kind, and those that clearly do not. The criterion was the median years of schooling reported for each occupation: those with 16 years or more were placed in the "college" group. Weighted by population, the jobs requiring college degrees accounted for 68 per cent of the GED 5's in 1950 and 32 per cent in 1960. Actually, the GED-5 jobs usually associated with college graduates increased, but the shift of many "non-college" jobs up to this level (and their increase) was responsible for the decline in the proportion of "college" jobs between 1950 and 1960.

The issue here is decidedly important in light of the considerable growth in middle-level jobs in our economy, jobs that seem to require several elements of what sociologist Erving Goffman terms "the presentation of self in everyday life." Insurance adjusters, to take just one example, must present themselves in their workaday lives as middle-class archetypes, a requirement that, willy nilly, tends to be confounded with concepts of general educational development. The gloss is an important product of the educational process in America,[21] and in a transitional period these new and expanding occupations (especially in the so-called service sector), not surpris-

---

[21] The experience of one major insurance company, as we shall see in Chapter V, indicates that there is no significant correlation between the gloss of its salesman, thus conceived, and the dollar values of their sales.

ingly, are likely to be miscast in terms of their "true" educational requirements.

In any case, Version 5 represents a final attempt to strike a balance between theory and practice by redistributing GED-5 jobs in two segments: the "non-college" segment is combined with the GED-4 level and the "college" segment with the GED 6's. (GED levels 1-3 remain matched with non-high-school graduates, as in the two previous versions.) Therefore, Version 5 represents a compromise among possible assumptions about the nature of job requirements. The totals indicate that there is a "surplus" of college graduates who presumably "drift down" to fill the deficit at the next lowest level, but this phenomenon seems confined to males. The near-perfect match between the supply and the demand for women college graduates seems to be due to the shift of teachers involved in the allocations of the GED 5's, a hypothesis that appears to square with relevant evidence. Among women, about three fourths of all GED-5 jobs defined in this fifth version as requiring college degrees were in teaching.

Otherwise, in this last version there is the same "move toward the middle" observed with respect to males in previous versions, while women are once again filling "deficits" in supply at the lowest level of jobs.

Conclusions

No one version of the data presented in this chapter is clearly superior to the others. In each case some assumptions are attractive and some are unacceptable. The problems in estimating the nature of the utilization of educated manpower in the United States by the "direct" approach are, at the very least, a good deal more complex than might be supposed from a reading of the earlier and ground-breaking studies, even allowing for their cautious stipulations concerning the adequacy of the data.

In the conceptually most attractive versions (3 and 5), there is a distinct drift of "better" educated people into "middle" level jobs and a reduction in the number of "less" educated people who move up into middle-level jobs in the decade covered by the data. The increase in educational requirements for middle-level jobs—which may not be gainsaid by reference to other versions that are concerned with whether the increases are "justified" by changes in the jobs themselves—may thus be taking place at some cost to a society that has historically prided itself on its mobility opportunities.

Of greater concern in the present context is the finding that it is not easier to locate useful estimates of "true" job requirements by the "direct" approach than by the more straightforward approaches considered in the previous chapter. The "direct" approach, however, does avoid the specific pitfalls encountered in efforts that are anchored in classical investment theory and leaves open a variety of ways for the consideration of employer "tastes," or prejudices. As we move between Versions 3 and 5, on the one hand, and the remaining versions, on the other, we can identify somewhat more clearly the nature of these tastes and, by making different assumptions, weigh their place in manpower equations. The questions that emerge from this exercise bear precisely upon this issue.

Granted that the USES estimates of trait requirements are reasonably good and that the *best* matches of supply and demand among the versions presented actually prevail in the economy, the next problem is to determine whether, if job requirements continue to change as they have in the past, educational achievements (supply) will in the *future* outdistance demand.

A related question is whether an "excess" of the supply over the demand in the economy for education will be absorbed to the advantage or disadvantage of the nation, the managers, and people of diverse educational backgrounds. If education is a formal credential of progressively less economic importance, a more serious question arises than whether the most educated people in our society are "utilized" in some economically meaningful way. For such a "credentialling" process isolates a significant population group—those with modest educational achievements—from the rest of American society. America, it may be argued (in either moral or economic terms), can afford such a development even less than it can afford to have disenchanted college graduates in its work force.

In the next chapter the problem of the absorption of educated manpower is considered briefly from a demographic point of view and then from the point of view of employers interviewed during the present study.

IV Demographic and Managerial Requirements

The vague misgivings one may have about the inventive indirect or "human capital" approaches to the identification of economic criteria for education are not completely or even largely dissipated by the employment of more direct methods. Thus myriad conceptual and methodological problems attended the efforts, described in the preceding chapter, to compute actual job requirements from trait analyses.

Nevertheless, the fact that such efforts to examine the supply of and "actual" demand for different levels of educated manpower are longitudinal in character is a source of their strength. Because the data are descriptive of two time periods, it was possible to examine the trends, presented in five different versions, that represent more or less conservative conceptions of present-day manpower policies and practices in America. Even the versions that correspond most closely to the *status quo*, and thus support the "education craze," contain some hints that the rising demand for workers with more elaborate educational credentials, in the short run, is in response to available supply rather than to long-unsatisfied organization needs, and that developments on the educational and employment fronts cannot be viewed with total equanimity.

In this chapter it is therefore appropriate to present, first, such demographic data as will provide clues to developments in the near future and, second, the relevant views of employers.

Educational Achievements and the Demands for an Educated Work Force

In making estimates of future trends in education and employment, an important issue is whether the rate of change in educational achievements will outdistance the change in educational requirements. The data on changes in educational achievements of the experienced labor force (Table IV-1) give one reason for pause, even assuming that all of the shifts in the occupational structure are "real" and significant.[1]

The data in Table IV-1 are based on the experienced civilian labor force, 14 years old or over, in each of three census years. In 1940, however, they do not include about 2.5 million workers, or about 5 per cent of the total, who were on public emergency work. This omission may be responsible for the fact that the decline in the lowest education group was greater in the second decade considered (1950–60) than in the first (1940–50). The only other striking difference is the smaller increase in the high-school-graduate group in the second decade. One can only speculate that as high-school graduation became a norm, a large increase from 1940 to 1950 resulted from the backlog—the pent-up demand, so to speak—left over from the depression; after 1950, the increase was expectedly somewhat less.

[1] How real these shifts are, and the precise magnitude of real *versus* pseudo shifts, is not easily established, as the analysis in Chapter III perhaps makes clear. The fact that educational achievement is sometimes combined with income in efforts to locate Americans in the "occupational structure" confuses this particular issue. See, for example, the strategy employed in Peter Blau and Otis Dudley Duncan, *The American Occupational Structure* (New York: Wiley, 1967).

TABLE IV-1

PERCENTAGE CHANGE IN YEARS OF SCHOOL COMPLETED
BY THE EXPERIENCED CIVILIAN LABOR FORCE,
1940–50, 1950–60, 1940–60

Years of School Completed	Percentage change		
	1940ª–50	1950–60	1940ª–60
8 years or less	−9.3	−14.4	−22.4
1–3 years high school	27.8	30.4	66.7
High-school graduate	44.0	32.7	91.1
1–3 years college	49.5	46.2	118.6
College graduate	47.7	47.5	117.8
Total labor force	12.9	14.8	29.6

ª The 1940 data exclude 5 per cent of the experienced civilian labor force, who were on public emergency work.

SOURCE: 1940 Census, *Occupational Characteristics,* Table 3; 1950 Census, *Occupational Characteristics* (Special Report P-E No. 1B), Table 10; 1960 Census, *Occupational Characteristics* (Subject Report PC[2]-7A), Table 9.

Another interesting feature presented by the table is the maintenance of parity in the growth of both parts of the college population, those with less than four years and those with four or more years of higher education. In each decade, each group increased by almost half. For the two decades, growth was about 118 per cent, compared to 91 per cent for high-school graduates.

If we consider the changing educational achievements of the total population in such a way that the cumulative effects on the base used in percentaging are eliminated by regarding equivalent but nonoverlapping subpopulations, the results are even more startling, as Table IV-2 shows.[2]

[2] The changes are still more dramatic when data for the civilian labor force rather than the total population are used as the basis for comparisons. Since labor-force participation rates are continually changing (upward), the total population is used here as the more relevant base for present purposes. It may be usefully noted, for example, that "about one third of the labor-force expansion between 1961 and 1968 was among women 25 years old and over, most of whom were married, and over half was made up of youth 16 to 24 years of age." U.S. Department of Labor, *Manpower Report of the President* (Washington: Government Printing Office, 1969), p. 50.

TABLE IV-2

PERCENTAGE DISTRIBUTION OF POPULATION 18-24 YEARS OF AGE, BY YEARS OF SCHOOL COMPLETED, BY SEX, 1940, 1950, AND 1960

Years of School Completed	Males			Females			Total		
	1940	1950	1960	1940	1950	1960	1940	1950	1960
8 years or less	34.0	26.0	15.1	28.8	19.3	11.2	31.3	22.6	13.2
1-3 years high school	26.8	26.5	27.2	25.7	25.6	26.5	26.3	26.0	26.9
High-school graduate	28.0	30.3	36.5	34.9	40.3	44.3	31.5	35.4	40.4
1-3 years college	8.7	14.0	16.8	8.3	11.4	14.6	8.5	12.7	15.6
College graduate	2.5	3.2	4.4	2.3	3.4	3.4	2.4	3.3	3.9
Total	100.0	100.0	100.0	100.0	100.0	100.0	100.0	100.0	100.0
Number (in millions)	(8.1)	(7.5)	(7.6)	(8.4)	(7.9)	(7.9)	(16.5)	(15.4)	(15.5)

Source: 1960 Census, Vol. 1, *Characteristics of the Population*, Part 1, U.S. Summary, table 173; 1950 Census, Vol. II, *Characteristics of the Population*, Part 1, U.S. Summary, table 114; 1940 data from 1950 Census, *ibid.*

The important question for the future is whether the increase in college population will begin to level off (parallel to the observed trend for high-school graduates), or whether the growth will continue. The trends described in Tables IV-1 and 2 are not likely to be reversed. Indeed, they are likely to be intensified. The expansion of community colleges, the boom in junior colleges, and the college building efforts of recent years will add to other forces that contribute to an increase in the numbers of citizens who will, in the future, achieve higher educations.

That the growth has continued in the nine years since the last census is already clear. The effects of ever-increasing school enrollments among a larger school-age population indicate that by 1975, about 66 per cent of workers 25 years old or over will have had at least four years of high school, and 15 per cent will have graduated from college.[3]

> By 1975, the adult work force . . . will include as many college graduates as those with 8 years of schooling or less . . . in 1959, college graduates as a group in the work force were but one third the size of the other component.[4]

The Problem of a Growing Supply of Educated People

It is neither unreasonable nor irrelevant to ask, in light of the prospects these trends imply, whether education in the future might offer Americans at each level of educational achievement something less than the expectations engendered by educational experience. It was this issue that concerned Seymour

---

[3] Denis F. Johnston, "Education of Adult Workers in 1975," *Special Labor Force Report No. 95* (Washington: Government Printing Office, 1968), p. 12.

[4] *Ibid.*, p. 10.

Harris twenty years ago in the study to which reference was made earlier:

> . . . *in the light of our college graduates' vocational expectations the numbers are, and will be increasingly excessive* . . . a large proportion of the potential college students within the next twenty years are doomed to disappointment after graduation, as the number of coveted openings will be substantially less than the numbers seeking them.[5]

Professor Harris's gloom has often been cited as a classic case of the clouded crystal ball. It is conceivable that he was simply prematurely anxious; it is even more likely that, in the two decades since he wrote his book, large numbers of jobs have been "educationally upgraded."

Some support for this conclusion may be found in a recent monograph on education based on the 1960 census. The analysis, which is confined to white males aged 35 to 54 years, subdivided into nine major occupational groups commonly used in the census, shows that "the association of education and occupation has been moderate but is declining." (Gamma = .52 in 1940, .50 in 1950, and .39 in 1960).[6] The study then seeks to determine whether the demand for more-educated workers rose because the supply increased, or whether demand stimulated the growth of the supply. Subdividing the rise in educational attainment into a component due to increases in educational attainment within occupational groups shows that upgrading within groups is by far the more important:

> Overall, about 85 per cent of the rise in educational attainment may be attributed to increased educational levels *within* occu-

---

[5] Seymour Harris, *The Market for College Graduates* (Cambridge: Harvard University Press, 1949), p. 64. Emphasis in original.

[6] John K. Folger and Charles B. Nam, *Education of the American Population*, 1960 Census Monograph (Washington: Government Printing Office, 1967), p. 169.

pations, and only 15 per cent to shifts in the occupational structure from occupations requiring less education to occupations requiring more. . . .

Only at the extremes of the attainment distribution (that is, for college graduates and for persons with no education) was as much as one half the change in educational attainment attributable to shifts between occupations.[7]

Because the occupational categories were so broad, the authors, while supporting the view that "the educational levels of workers in various occupations do change and reflect the 'supply' of persons as well as the occupational demand," conclude that "how much of the change reflects increased skill requirements . . . and how much is due to the availability of better-educated persons for the same jobs cannot be finally determined from these data."[8]

It is clear, however, that recent increments of college graduates have spread out into the middle levels of the occupational structure. Between 1950 and 1960, the labor force gained about a half-million *more* male college graduates than were required to maintain 1950 educational attainment levels. Only 12 per cent of these (a little over 100,000) were added to the professions; about 225,000 went into managerial occupations, 100,000 into sales occupations, and the remainder (75,000) were scattered through the other occupations. Most of the additional males with a high-school diploma were concentrated in the craftsman and operative categories.[9]

If 1975 distributions for males remain the same as obtained in 1960, "there will be about 3.1 million more high-school graduates, 850,000 more persons with some college education, and 3.3 million more college graduates than will be required. . . ."[10] Even if the upgrading trend continues within

[7] *Ibid.*, pp. 171–72. Emphasis added.
[8] *Ibid.*, p. 173.
[9] *Ibid.*, p. 175.
[10] *Ibid.*, p. 174.

occupational groups, the prospects for a greater rate of absorption of college graduates into the professions is unlikely (since the proportion is already high). The large projected increase, perforce, will have to be absorbed in "managerial, sales, clerical, and some craftsmen occupations."[11]

These data imply that we may be able to absorb more highly educated people by redefining the requirements for employment, if not the job itself, and thus, in the fashion of Humpty Dumpty, make the content of work what we say it is.[12] In effect, this was demonstrated in Chapter III in the presentation of five different versions of the "match" between job requirements and educational achievements. Those who take an optimistic view of the match, at present and for the near future, should pause long enough to examine some possible consequences:

1. The "unemployed college man" is probably a "spectre." Nevertheless, disequilibrium may set in. The College Placement Council estimated, for example, that from 1967 to 1968, the decline in the number of jobs offered youths leaving college was 2 per cent for graduates with a bachelor's degree, 19 per cent for those with a master's degree, and 12 per cent for Ph.D.'s.[13] It is not possible to determine whether this a cyclical or a secular phenomenon, but it does demonstrate that the demand curve may well take a direction other than up.

2. More serious is the possibility of increasing "underemployment" of college men—and women. There is a real question whether middle-level white-collar jobs, those that have shown the greatest proliferation, actually make suitable use of their incumbents' preparation. In setting the requirements for work, it is well to keep in mind that "people *normally* operate within the bounds of a great deal of intellectual

---

[11] *Ibid.*, p. 176.

[12] Humpty Dumpty also said, "When I make a word do a lot of work like that, I always pay it extra."

[13] College Placement Council, *Salary Survey, Final Report*, June, 1968 (Bethlehem, Pa.: The Council, 1968), p. 1.

slack" so that it is difficult to measure the effects of marginal increments of knowledge.[14] The noneconomic factors[15] of managerial policy and the organization of work play an important mediating role between input and output; while these may act to improve efficiency, they may also involve unanticipated costs, as we shall see in later chapters.

Apropos of such anticipated costs, Professor Harris's statement about expectations becomes a real-life issue. At a recent high-level conference concerned with the prospect of collective bargaining among scientific and technical employees and professionals, the conferees agreed that "automation and computerization are eating away at the decision-making powers of these workers," and that "as their numbers increase, the uniqueness of the individual and his talents will decrease."[16] The problem, then, has several parts—the potential for actual underutilization, the workers' perceptions of how the facts fulfill their expectations, and the costs to employers and workers alike.

3. The most serious consequence of the educational upgrading of work opportunities is already with us—the displacement of a significant population at the other end of the labor force, who must compete for jobs once held by people of modest educational achievement and with people whose educational achievements have gone up. Neither the "human capital" approach nor the approach whereby educational requirements are computed directly helps to determine where

[14] Harvey Leibenstein, "Allocative Efficiency vs. 'X-Efficiency'," *American Economic Review*, LVI (1966), p. 405.

[15] For a discussion of one aspect of this issue, see Armen A. Alchian and Reuben A. Kessel, "Competition, Monopoly and the Pursuit of Pecuniary Gain," in National Bureau of Economic Research, *Aspects of Labor Economics* (Princeton: Princeton University Press, 1962), pp. 157–75, in which the authors note managerial tastes for "prettier-than-usual" secretaries, for example, in place of profit maximization.

[16] Conference on "Collective Bargaining and Professional Responsibility," sponsored by the AFL-CIO and conducted by the University of Illinois Institute for Labor and Industrial Relations, *AFL-CIO News*, July 13, 1968.

narrow economic necessities with respect to education leave off in the production process and where the sociological advantages of educational requirements to organizations, individuals, and society begin. There *may* be sociopsychological benefits to people and organizations stemming from diplomas and degrees, but these benefits must be seen in a perspective that takes account of the consequences for the "uncredentialed."

Most programs designed to deal with this problem have been geared to helping unemployed workers compete in the labor market by improving their qualifications. In the meantime, we reward the highly educated with superior incomes on the grounds of their productive contribution. If a man cannot meet the educational standards, his work is, by the definition of his income, or lack of income, less productive. Like Petruchio, we have been willing to accord those at the bottom neither the beef of a living and steady wage nor the mustard of a share in the over-all gains of the economy. Petruchio, however, had only to tame a shrew; we have to deal with the question of equity for a whole society.

As the specific work activities of men are further and further removed from a discernible end product, it becomes more and more difficult to assign each one his fair share of the proceeds, and the decision is particularly complex at the middle skill levels. We have chosen to allocate income largely according to educational achievement. As a result, the version of the relationship between supply and demand that requires improvement in educational achievements and upgrading of jobs to move at the same rate is not without its price, even if we put aside the problem of "underutilized" college graduates.

There are, of course, those who see the matter differently, who see far many more advantages and benefits than costs accruing to a society in which the educational credentials for jobs are upgraded beyond those necessary for "adequate" performance. The "human capital" writers, for example, offer abundant arguments in favor of present trends. One economist, in enumerating a host of so-called external benefits of education that redound to individuals as well as to the nation, includes such "social benefits" as the simplifications in income-tax collection that an educated population makes possible![17] By lengthening the list, one can, with only a little imagination, make investments in education pay off handsomely indeed. According to such logic, *by definition* there can be no "excess" education with respect to society.

Another argument maintains that earning differentials confirm the benefits employers receive from the greater educational achievements of individual employees; the pressures of the marketplace will enjoin the employer to use his workers with maximum efficiency and to recruit the members of his work force with an eye to his revenues. In such a formulation, however, as we noted earlier in connection with efforts to identify economic criteria for education by rate of return analysis, there is considerable overlap between *explanans* and *explanandum*. The problem is formulated in such a way that antecedent assumptions affirm that which is to be proved.

If, in fact, excess education is obviated by assuming the economic rationality of wage differentials, it is sensible to look behind the troublesome methods, direct and indirect, that have so far been discussed, and to determine whether managers themselves can assure us that educational credentials are worth what economists say they are.

Economists do not deal with individual firms when they work with theoretical apparatuses constructed for purposes of examining the concomitant variations in aggregated economic data, and some have expressed reasonable doubts about the utility (*i.e.*, the marginal costs) of information gathered from

[17] Burton A. Weisbrod, *External Benefits of Public Education: An Economic Analysis* (Princeton: Industrial Relations Section, Department of Economics, Princeton University, 1964), pp. 24–26. It would be interesting to contemplate a series of tax reforms which, while making taxes more equitable, would also reduce the complexities facing taxpayers.

practicing businessmen for such analytical purposes.[18] An examination of business behavior, however, may give the theoretician precious little comfort. Indeed, one might wish, in light of a number of studies of policy-making in the nation's great enterprises, that the jump from theory to policy might be undertaken more gingerly than economists suggest.

Educational Credentials in Managerial Perspective

Interviews with highly placed executives responsible for personnel policies revealed the same bewildering behavior concerning educational credentials that has been endlessly recounted by social scientists who have patrolled the shops and offices of business and government ever since the days of the classic experiments at the Hawthorne works of the Western Electric Corporation. These discussions with managers evoked the same question-begging responses that were obtained in investigations of business decision-making, including pricing decisions and decisions to subcontract. Two of the author's colleagues reported that some of the companies they investigated make only rough cost calculations in "make-or-buy" decisions, while fully 40 per cent make no calculations whatever.[19] In fact, with a few obvious changes in wording, the following description by three Brookings Institution economists of pricing decisions in "a representative sample of large enterprises" could serve to describe the findings of our interviews with ten large employers.[20]

18 See Fritz Machlup, "Theories of the Firm: Behavioral, Managerial and Marginalist," *American Economic Review*, LVII (1967), 1–33.

19 Leonard Sayles and Margaret Chandler, *Contracting Out: A Study of Management Decision Making* (New York: Columbia University Graduate School of Business, 1959), pp. 36ff.

20 The "sample" included three of the four largest rubber companies; one large bank; one hospital supply company; one packaging company; one of

It was evident that most of the executives with whom interviews were conducted did not ordinarily concern themselves with pricing details; instances appeared in which they were not intimately aware of how their products were priced. Even those who were quite familiar with company policy in the pricing area were among those who could not illustrate the policy by a detailed follow through of particular price decisions. The fact that in some of the companies there was a gulf between the top officials and the price makers is in itself significant.

Even where the people doing the pricing tended to have certain staff information placed before them while making up their minds, whether and just how the information was taken into consideration often remained obscure. . . . Repeatedly reference was made to the "art" or "feel" of pricing rather than observance of a formula.[21]

Personnel and manpower decisions are *made*, to be sure, but the histories of such decisions are little more than hazy and unsubstantiated recollections of the "it-seemed-like-a-good-idea" variety. Our sample of firms is as small as it is simply because the responses to probes were so drearily similar from firm to firm that there seemed to be no benefit to be gained from expanding the effort. Our effort at interviews was therefore terminated early in the research.

Considerable manpower planning was undertaken in these firms with respect to executive personnel: like most large companies, they have a variety of executive development programs, either in association with universities or within the company, or in combination of the two. These programs range from short "exposure" to prolonged residency, during which a host of issues and techniques bearing on "human rela-

the biggest textile companies; one of the "big five" steel companies; one large, diversified textile company, and two small textile manufacturers. While abundant notes were compiled, no effort was made to treat the responses as formal "survey research" data.

[21] Abraham D. H. Kaplan, Joel B. Dirlam, and Robert Lanzilotti, *Pricing in Big Business: A Case Approach* (Washington: Brookings Institution, 1958), p. 5.

tions" and macro-economic policy problems are covered, with excursions in between into "systems analysis" and "sensitivity training." The latter is designed to make managers more "interpersonally competent" and to modify their behavior so that their peers and subordinates will experience a heightened sense of "self-actualization."

Most executive development efforts are organized around the principle that participants are drawn from the ranks of the nation's college graduates, whose educational backgrounds prepare them for sophisticated efforts calculated to make them better leaders and decision makers. All the spokesmen made bold statements about the value to their firms of college-educated men, and even those with graduate degrees, although these firms all had highly placed personnel with more modest credentials. On the face of it, the claims make sense. There can be no gainsaying the fact that a large firm might suffer if its executives were politically naive, organizationally heavy-handed, or intellectually uninformed about the complexities of the American economy.

Efforts to obtain data comparing the performance of better- and less-educated executives, however, ended in failure. In an extended conversation with one personnel executive and his assistant, it developed that they had a series of profiles, including graphs, portraying the accomplishments of their executives with respect, for example, to promotions, sales records, bonuses, and the like. These profiles, a few of which we were privileged to examine, had not been systematically analyzed, however, and it was impossible to make any judgments about the relationships between the personal traits and the performance records of these men.

Since the profiles were neatly compiled and readily accessible, the two executives were asked about the value of educational credentials in selection. The answers did not appear to be based on even casual perusal of the available data. In the matter of the *number* of people to which the profiles and our conversation referred, the respondents made incredibly divergent estimates; one said 800 men, the other said 300! It was clear that *no* effort had been made to consider the issue of educational credentials and equally clear that the issues of people, work, and even efficiency were negligible in the minds of these executives.

In this and other companies, however, it was readily acknowledged that the turnover of young executives varies only slightly; there is an average loss of *half* of all college graduates within the first five years of employment. Manpower planning at this organizational level was "therefore" uniformly informed by this "fact of life," as it was called; twice as many college graduates were recruited as were "needed."

There was, of course, abundant testimony concerning the worth of college graduates, and in this testimony the unifying theme was the diligence and "stick-to-it-iveness" of a young man who can endure four years of college. The college degree was consistently taken as a badge of the holder's stability and was apparently a highly prized characteristic of young recruits. Most of the respondents made it perfectly plain that the content of a college program mattered a good deal less than the fact of successful completion of studies. The poise and self-assurance of college graduates received considerable attention as well.

One highly successful company is staffed at the junior executive level by a unique group of college graduates; its college recruiters select many candidates from among those who have worked in men's haberdasheries catering to collegiate customers, on or near campuses, in the belief that these young fellows combine a highly desirable set of appetites, skills, and styles. Recruiters from this company also look for vacant seats on airplanes next to well-appointed young men whose college background can be inferred from the rings they wear. These airborne campaigns, an executive assuringly pointed

out, were highly productive, although consultations with a.
designer of occult psychological tests were the closest these
executives came to scientific investigation.

When questioned about the high turnover rates of young
college graduates, nearly all the respondents answered im-
pressionistically, by outlining the reasons supplied in termina-
tion interviews and in occasional and rather crude "career
follow-ups" by the personnel officers. Many, they said, left
simply because they were unhappy with their locations, or because their families had made poor adjustments to their en-
vironments. But others left because they felt that they were
not getting ahead and that their jobs, by their standards, were
insufficiently challenging.

Such attitudes were typically written off, however, as the
reactions of "kids who want too much" or who "think they
are better than they are" or "who haven't yet learned the facts
of life, that you have to bide your time." In only one company did the jobs to which college men were assigned during
their early careers sound like responsible positions. This company, in the packaging industry, frequently assigns new grad-
uate-business-school alumni to jobs as assistant plant managers
or as highly placed supervisory personnel with major responsibilities for developing the marketing, financial, or other programs of a plant. Their turnover levels were appreciably
lower than the 50-per-cent figure given by the other respondents.

Another company, mindful of the increasingly simplified
nature of the production processes in their plants, had experimented with the recruitment of American Indians whose educational backgrounds were modest by any standard. The
executive who recounted the story claimed, with justifiable
pride, that the program had been successful but indicated that
it would take a great deal of work, combing "dead" piece-rate
payment files, to determine the benefits to production of his
company's exciting venture in social experimentation.

One hopes that the effort was indeed a success; perhaps executives get their rewards in heaven when they thus walk on the side of the angels. The researcher, however, must wait for the evidence. An invitation to look at the raw data was coupled with intimations of the company's inconvenience, a forthright statement that race and ethnic data were privileged, and intimidating descriptions of the magnitude of the coding problem that would have to be surmounted. The same company, in the meantime, has computerized all nonpersonnel data, but personnel data were ignored in accordance with the pervasive logic (implicit in all the interviews) that one of the biggest cost areas—personnel—is amenable to neither study nor influence.

The other companies had also ignored the question of education and its economic benefits and had conducted very little experimentation in connection with hiring requirements, except where signs of good faith were needed for a local, regional, or national job or poverty campaign. One company, for example, in collaboration with researchers from the University of Notre Dame's Department of Sociology, was examining the benefits of hiring ex-convicts. Virtually all of the companies belonged to business associations that sought jobs for "hard-core" unemployed, but headquarters personnel, perhaps wisely, discussed these efforts rather elliptically. The public press, meanwhile, continues to suggest that these efforts have been fragmentary in nature and more often than not marginal to the concerns of the corporate manpower specialists in high places.[22]

In only one company were the educational characteristics of manpower—at all job levels—routinely reported to personnel and other company officials. In the East Chicago offices of

[22] The foregoing is intended not to detract from these undertakings but merely to imply that the problems are a good deal more serious than these efforts can handle. For encouraging information see Ivar Berg, "Help Wanted," *Columbia University Forum*, III (Fall, 1964), 10-15.

Inland Steel, manpower planners *apologized* for having data that were already one week old! And they were surprised to learn that other companies did not have equivalent computer print-out for planning purposes.

In the other companies, educational data were filed away in personnel applications and employment forms, never to distract executives from their determined efforts to "improve the quality of our people." To a man, the respondents assured us that diplomas and degrees were a good thing, that they were used as screening devices by which undesirable employment applicants could be identified, and that the credentials sought were indicators of personal commitment to "good middle-class values," industriousness, and seriousness of purpose, as well as salutary personal habits and styles. One executive pointed out that with only two people conducting interviews of job applicants, "we needed something to cut the sheer numbers down to what the personnel office could handle." To the executive, this logic was self-evident.

The interviews produced a picture of the results of this logic; most (not all!) of the respondents were confounded by questions that cast any doubt on the managerial wisdom underlying the raising of educational requirements. Although his term was not employed, a version of Marx's notion of the surplus army of labor was regularly invoked in a favorable way, the idea being that unemployment, especially among younger job applicants, makes it possible to take advantage of the self-selection and social-selection processes that differentiate between the desirable and undesirable—*i.e.*, the better- and less-educated—additions to a work force. The "loose" labor market of the '50's, then, was considered a boon in the personnel offices of these companies.

Uneasy about logic that purports to be "self-evident," one pursues the issue even less productively in specific terms than in generalities. Thus it turned out that *none* of the companies had considered educational achievements in studies of turnover, absenteeism, productivity, grievance patterns, output "restriction," terminations "for cause," unionization interests, job satisfaction, supervisors' evaluations, or any other directly or indirectly relevant dimension of work behavior. This, of course, may be due in part to the fact that few companies had even undertaken studies of these problems, although all the companies admitted that they suffered organizationally from one or more of them.

Every company had instituted complex personnel benefit programs, morale-building programs, human-relations activities, or combinations of these efforts, to reduce costly problems and increase productivity. Despite this, most of the headquarters offices had relatively little knowledge of the personnel issues facing the local managers of plants and subsidiaries, or of the efforts undertaken, if any, to resolve them. "We are quite decentralized from that point of view," was not an unusual response to probes calculated to determine whether the variances in a problem area could in fact, as was implied, be attributed to "lower-quality" employees.

To be sure, people responsible for decisions to hire personnel gave reasons for raising educational requirements in companies that encouraged, ordered, or merely tolerated such practices: "Better-educated people are more promotable." Like college alumni, high-school graduates, by virtue of their staying in school rather than by virtue of their particular learning experiences or skills, were considered simply "better" and more likely, more able, and more intelligent prospects.

The promotability argument had an attractive ring—what teacher could fail to hope that he had made at least *that* contribution to the regiments of people that pass through his fumbling hands? Once again, however, the argument was unsupported by any evidence that better-educated people compare favorably with their less educated peers who started at some given point on the organization ladder. The fact that better-educated people in almost *any given job category* in these firms were *younger* than their peers suggests that the better-educated had started higher on the ladder when they joined the firm, and that any correlation of rank with education would probably be the substantially tautological results of recruiting and assignment strategies.

Job Requirements and Employer Practices

Discouraged by repeated confrontations with the self-fulfilling prophesies that appeared to be as rampant among employers as among the economists who accept the rates of return on education as a measure of its economic efficiency, we turned to published studies and to analyses of such raw data as were generously provided by the handful of employers who shared our suspicions about the wisdom of using educational credentials as a screening device.

The "quality" argument, in fine, had not been impressive; in the absence of data, neither were arguments that jobs were changing so fast in content as to require better-educated people. The trait study discussed in the previous chapter had already suggested that educational achievements were changing much more rapidly than jobs, however much concession is made to technological and other influences on work, a finding that induced cautious interpretations about the "automation revolution" to which respondents made reference.

Other data increased our suspicions that there may be a significant margin of education that goes beyond what employers need even for *good* plant and corporate performance. In this connection, the National Industrial Conference Board's exploratory study of job vacancies in New York's Monroe County (which includes Rochester) reports that educational requirements vary with the academic year and appear to be geared to semester endings and commencement exercises:

The proportion of vacancies which did not require high school graduation was much higher in August than in February or May [1965]. In August, about 3,900 openings, or 45 per cent of the total, required less than 12 years of schooling. The corresponding percentages in February and May were 37 and 35, respectively.

The relative importance of vacancies requiring exactly 12 years of schooling declined sharply from May to August, thus returning to a level similar to that existing in February.[23]

The National Industrial Conference Board, a not-unfriendly critic of business decision-making, is probably right when it concludes from its data that

. . . it seems reasonable to attribute these changes to recruiting in May for recent high-school graduates. Employers may have tailored their requirements to match the qualifications of this new supply of labor.[24]

A study based on the USES trait requirements, the same type of achievements-requirements analysis reported in Chapter III, further supports this somewhat skeptical view of corporate practices.[25] While the authors carefully eschewed *any* translation of general educational development into years of education, they did compare all the 1956 and 1966 trait requirements delineated by the USES (including GED) as

[23] "Measuring Job Vacancies: The Third Survey," *The Conference Board Record* (New York: NICB, November, 1965), p. 31.

[24] *Ibid.*, pp. 31–32. The summary study in this series shows essentially the same results but the authors do not comment on the meaning of the calendar shifts in demand for better-educated workers. See John G. Myers and Daniel Creamer, *Measuring Job Vacancies: Studies in Business Economics,* No. 97 (New York: NICB, 1967), pp. 49–51.

[25] Morris A. Horowitz and Irwin L. Herrnstadt, "Changes in the Skill Requirements of Occupations in Selected Industries," in "The Employment Impact of Technological Change," Appendix Volume II, *Technology and the American Economy* (Report of the National Commission on Technology, Automation and Economic Progress, Washington: Government Printing Office, 1966), pp. 225–87.

well as the detailed job descriptions for five industries. They concluded that the over-all or net change in the skill requirements was remarkably small, especially considering that their study covered a quarter-century (1940–65). "There was considerable change in occupational requirements and content, but on balance, it was inconsequential or inconclusive with respect to over-all skill levels."[26]

The jobs examined in the study by Professors Horowitz and Herrnstadt were predominantly blue-collar. In another study, by the New York State Department of Labor, an effort was made to compare the (minimum) requirements and the (ideal) preferences of employers regarding education for jobs in 15 technical occupational groups, on the one hand, with the achievements of nearly 150,000 individuals who had worked in these occupations in New York State in 1962. The data show that employer preferences for college degrees ran ahead of the number of technicians with undergraduate degrees in only two of the 15 occupational categories. The educational achievements of technicians exceeded not only the minimum requirements but also the preferences of employers (with respect to degrees from technical institutes) in 10 of the 15 occupational groups. It is not possible to determine from the data whether the "excess" of institute graduates constitutes a trade-off against the "shortage" of college graduates, with shortage here defined as the workers' college achievements balanced against the employers' preferences.[27]

The popular assumption, supported by employers and, to some degree, economists, that widespread technological

---

[26] *Ibid.*, p. 287. In a preliminary report on the training of tool-and-die makers, the same authors conclude that performance (as rated by foremen) did not vary significantly among workers with different training paths. Furthermore, completing a given training path was not a prerequisite to success in the occupation. Morris A. Horowitz and Irwin L. Herrnstadt, "An Evaluation of the Training of Tool and Die Makers," Preliminary Report (Boston: Northeastern University, 1969).

[27] *Technical Manpower in New York State* (New York: State of New York Department of Labor, 1964), Vol. I, p. 47.

change in America is responsible for the demand for better-educated workers gained even less support from a recent study of the effect of technology.[28] From their data on workers' educational attainment and changes in output per worker (taken as a rough index of technological change) by industry, by sex, and by occupation, the authors infer that

> . . . there is little, if any, relationship between changes in educational level [1950–60] and changes in output per worker. In those industries in which output per worker increased by less than 2 per cent annually (and employment increased under 15 per cent), 77 per cent of the employed men in 1950 had not completed high school, as compared with 72 per cent in 1960. At the other extreme, among those industries in which output per worker increased by 4 per cent or more per year (and employment increased by under 15 per cent) the proportion of dropouts fell from 83 per cent in 1950 to 76 per cent in 1960.[29]

Such data might well be *necessary*, but they are not *sufficient* to overturn the formidable body of beliefs in support of the rising demands of employers for educated manpower. It does no injustice to the authors' imaginative efforts to point out that their use of "output per worker" as an indicator of technological change begs important questions.

In order for such data to contribute to a *sufficient* argument, controls would have to be introduced for a number of potentially important contributing factors. One would wish to know whether, as might be likely, capital intensity is higher in industries with greater rates of increase in output per worker. Additional factors—such as the increasing educational achievements of *managers*—might vary a good deal from companies and industries with high rates of increase in productivity to companies and industries with low rates. When there

[28] A. J. Jaffe and Joseph Froomkin, *Technology and Jobs: Automation in Perspective* (New York: Praeger, 1968), pp. 85–97.

[29] *Ibid.*, p. 88.

are methodological obstacles to any clear-cut resolution, as is often the case, the conventional wisdom enjoys its alliance with attractive logic; its critics, however, are burdened with the chore of contesting the logic with data that are all too scarce.

In the remaining chapters of this book, we consider some of these data. They have been culled from the literature and re-analyzed, or they have been made available by managers of public agencies and private corporations. They permit extensive if not intensive examination of educational credentials in relation to performance in the workplace.

V Educational Achievements and Worker Performance

The search for evidence to give weight to economic arguments supporting the use of educational credentials for jobs has not been conspicuously successful. Aggregated data on income and education, favored in economists' researches, raise many more questions than they answer. The problems inherent in the economists' apparatus are compounded by those of a more strictly logical nature, problems that are more typically begged for analytical purposes than confronted in the simplifying assumptions of a general theoretical approach to reality.

The efforts of manpower and job analysts to identify the "real" educational requirements are of similarly problematical value; the difficulties of distinguishing employer *tastes* from employers' functional *needs* are in no wise eliminated by the use of the U.S. Employment Service's descriptions of jobs. These descriptions, while apparently based on today's practices, are themselves informed by preferences generated in the marriage of yesterday's labor-market conditions with prejudices honored too well by time. Thus margins of choice with respect to manpower utilization remain open to employers after technological determinants and the sorting process of market forces have shaped a firm's occupational structure.

And managers, upon whom there are strong pressures to be guided by evidence, usually offer little more than assertions in support of practices the benefits of which are assumed.

An alternative method is to examine the actual performance of workers in identical or similar jobs whose educational backgrounds are different to determine whether differential educational achievements might be related to differences in organizationally relevant behavior. It is to this point and to the related question of job attitudes that this chapter and the next two chapters are directed.

The chore is not a simple one, a fact for which many of us may be grateful. Indeed, there are few standards against which the adequacy of most employed Americans can be judged. Our occupational efforts are frequently bound up inextricably with the work of others in the production of goods —and, increasingly, services.

Where a man's (or woman's) work *is* extricable from the efforts of others, the results are substantially influenced by forces over which the individual has little control. It is a poor field representative whose declining sales record cannot be attributed to market conditions, and an unusual one who successfully competes with the advertising agency's claims to the credit for a rising sales curve! The acceptance by many Americans of the seniority principle in organizations is perhaps the best barometer of the implicit effect of these facts of complex industrial-bureaucratic life in America. In the absence of clear performance standards, most of us will choose job tenure as an indicator of capability and settle for the arbitrary seniority rule in preference to managerial definitions of the good worker. Where a man's contribution to an organization's work is not readily distinguishable, managerial judgments may be distrusted as whimsical, prejudicial, or both.

To be entirely convincing, of course, a comparison of the work performance of better-educated and less educated people would have to be systematic and statistically valid. Accordingly, one would prefer data that are representative of all occupations, and of all the people in these occupations, juxtaposed with all relevant dimensions of performance. It would also be desirable to be able to control in the data for other worker characteristics and attitudes to the extent that these influence worker performance, and also to control for managerial competence and an array of other factors that impinge upon employee behavior.

The data reported in the following pages fall far short of these requirements, but they are more than just suggestive of the truth. The cumulative weight of piecemeal evidence, after all, may be taken as a significant clue to truths that are not otherwise to be apprehended, and it is in this spirit that the materials are presented. Some of them are taken from previously published studies, but most were collected and analyzed in the course of the present investigation.

Blue-Collar Workers

In the first of the field investigations, data were collected in 1967 on the productivity, turnover, and absenteeism of 585 former and present female workers in a multi-plant Mississippi textile manufacturing company. We found that educational achievement was *inversely* related to performance thus conceived. Thus, where 57 per cent of the long-tenure employees had ten or more years of schooling, the figure for short-tenure employees was 71 per cent; the statistical probability that the observed difference would occur by chance is 5 in 100.

The data with respect to educational achievement correlated with productivity, which in this company could be measured accurately from piecework earnings, and absenteeism were somewhat less clear, but they gave no support to the contention that educational requirements are a useful screening device in blue-collar employee selection. The education of high producers did not differ from that of low producers to any statistically significant degree, although the *less* productive ones were slightly *better* educated. It is worth noting that the results can be generalized to the entire company since the groups about which the findings are drawn were constructed from a random 50-per-cent sample of over 1,000 former and nearly 850 present employees in the company's eight plants.[1] Since productivity data were examined only for long-tenure employees, the findings probably understate the magnitude of the inverse relationship between productivity and education.

In the same vein, there was no statistically significant relationship between educational achievement and absenteeism, another bugaboo of managers who are anxious to maintain smooth production schedules and continuous work flows, although there were slightly more high-school graduates among the "low" than the "high absentee" group.

In a comparable study of 762 workers in four departments of a Southern hosiery manufacturing plant, the same patterns were observed. Productivity and turnover were related to age, family stability, and a number of intra-organizational factors, but they were *not* associated with educational achievement among day-shift workers; education was *inversely* related to both measures of performance among employees on the night shift in this company.[2] We can speculate that better-educated workers were especially irritated by assignment to the night shift. Whatever the explanation, the employer did not benefit from having better-educated employees on either shift and actually lost out on the night shift with respect to productivity and turnover. Once again, the productivity measures were ac-

[1] For a more detailed analysis see Gordon Inskeep. "The Selection Process and Its Relationship to Productivity, Tenure, and Absenteeism among Garment Workers," unpublished doctoral dissertation, Columbia University, 1967, written under the author's supervision in connection with the present research.

[2] Michael Abramoff, "External Allocation, Socialization and Internal Allocation of Human Resources as Related to Performance," unpublished doctoral dissertation, Columbia University, 1968 written under the author's supervision in connection with the present research.

curate since they were constructed from piecework earnings for each employee.

It will be recalled, in our interviews regarding the "greater potential" of better-educated workers, that employers insisted that the elevation of education requirements reflects management's desires to build for the future by assuring a pool of labor from which promotions may be made. If their assumption is correct, we would expect to find that personnel who have been promoted are better educated than those who have not, especially in companies that are proud of the essential rationality of their manpower and personnel policies.

Although this expectation is not easily tested, we might well be skeptical of an intrinsically appealing analysis that protects its own flank by seeing long-term benefits in an approach to a short-run problem. In a parallel study, data were collected on the patterns of labor-force "attachment" among (1) installation-crew members in two privately owned urban utility companies, (2) workers in an auto assembly plant located on the periphery of one of America's great cities, and (3) nonmanagerial employees in two large urban department stores.[3] These data do not square with management's convenient rationale.

The patterns were substantially the same in all four employment settings; those of the installers are illustrative. In an effort to account for the promotion rates of these workers, educational achievement explained so few promotions that it could be discounted as a factor. The results were interesting, however, in that they offered some clues to the real nature of "organizational mobility," to borrow a barbarism from sociology, clues that are entirely consistent with the skeptical bias of the present study.

When the researcher who originally exploited the data examined the job titles in these four work settings, she dis-

[3] Marcia Freedman, *The Process of Work Establishment* (New York: Columbia University Press, 1969).

covered that although the titles were ordered into a pay scale, the resulting array did not correspond to a skill hierarchy except at the extreme ends of the wages continuum. It appears, then, that education may well be relevant to the "promotion potential" of workers in a shop or plant where title and pay changes reflect differences in job tasks and obligations, but it is not likely to be specifically relevant to promotions in settings where managers have developed a nominal hierarchy to legitimize wage differentials created by the numerous factors that operate in urban labor markets.

It is doubtful that the uncounted masses of Americans who are "promoted" each year are as easily fooled by nominal hierarchies as are some senior academics who conceive of occupational titles as ranks representing differential skills. Such ranks are merely included among the more socially significant rungs on the largely symbolic occupational "ladders." Assistant professors, we can be sure, will skillfully disabuse any academic coprolites who might challenge such a judgment.

Our strong suspicions about the nature of organizational careers, especially in the blue-collar fields, are not allayed by employers' assertions, especially in light of continuous efforts to rationalize and "bureaucratize" work. And theories purporting to account for labor unions' activities would be less than adequate if they did not assign a significant place to the occupational consequences of changes wrought by managers bent upon gaining benefits that accrue to "scale," specialization, and work simplification. In the four settings mentioned, education was a good predictor of initial salary and job title. But it will not surprise the reader to learn that seniority accounted for most of the promotions.

A final study, this time of "gray-collar" workers, gives further evidence concerning the specifics of educational achievement and worker behavior. Managers of a paper company (including a doctoral candidate on leave from his job as the

Director of Technical Personnel, who collected the data) were surprised that the wisdom of their preferences for better-educated technicians was not confirmed by relevant data.[4]

The data showed that short-tenure employees had a median of four and a half semesters of college training, while a matched sample of employees with longer service had completed only slightly more than three terms. It was an additional surprise to management that the longer-tenure (and therefore more valuable) employees scored substantially lower on an intelligence test, a test the personnel officials hoped would validate the practices of giving higher-scoring job candidates preferential treatment in placement.

There was, furthermore, no association between the educational attainments of these technicians and the evaluations they received from supervisory personnel, nor was there any association between education and absenteeism. And when the "reasons for leaving" given by former employees were reviewed, they revealed that over a third resigned well-paying jobs to return to school; another third left for jobs that offered higher starting salaries for their relatively advanced educational achievements.

These data and the observations of employers in our interviews suggest that better-educated people get ahead by changing jobs, and that their less educated peers stay behind and move into the higher-paying, if not always higher-skill, jobs vacated by employee turnover. Higher-skill jobs, meanwhile, are filled by the better-educated workers who have quit other employers.

There may, of course, be a higher wisdom than management's, according to which the materials discussed in this first section make a kind of sense. Perhaps turnover is simply a corrective process at the margins of the more rigid central

---

[4] These data were analyzed by Dr. Gordon Inskeep, now of Arizona State University, in connection with the work of a seminar conducted by the author at the Columbia University Graduate School of Business in 1966.

tendencies at work in a complex labor market; labor turnover is not all bad. And it is not likely that a perfect process of training, recruiting, placing, and paying workers will ever be devised. Nevertheless, we might hope that the value managers place on education as a screening device would be rewarded by a few *direct* associations between the achievements they prize and the productivity, attendance and loyalty they seek in their hired charges. It is probably fortunate that the ratios implied by these data are not included among those listed in annual reports since the wages paid to employees *are* directly correlated with education, a fact that may sadden proponents of efficiency in enterprise. Sadness gives way to anger among the spokesmen for those without academic credentials who continue to be told that their constituents "need more education."

White-Collar Workers

The facts are not more reassuring with respect to white-collar workers. An analysis of the merit pay increases awarded to over a hundred secretaries employed by one of the nation's largest magazine publishers revealed no discernible relationship between these rewards for performance and the educational achievements of the recipients who had attended various post-high-school programs but had not graduated from college.[5] Nor did any associations appear when the number rather than the amount of increases was considered. In fact, while a small number of college graduates received slightly more raises than the nongraduates, the education-evaluation data were otherwise *inversely* related.

[5] These data were made available by the magazine's personnel administrator and were analyzed by Dudley L. Post for a seminar conducted by the author in 1966.

A colleague who has been conducting studies of "debit agents" employed across the land by the Prudential Insurance Company has generously provided data on the sales accomplishments and education of each of four age groups among the 4,000 subjects that have been studied by Prudential's personnel researchers.[6] These data are especially interesting since they are broken down by the types of market in which the agents work, thereby holding constant a significant sales factor.

Three sets of progressively rigid sales and policy-retention rates for measuring the success of these agents were employed. The results were entirely anomalous when the agents' records were examined in connection with their educational achievements. The records of high-school graduates rarely differed by more than a few percentage points from those of comparably numerous college graduates of similar age operating in similar markets: sometimes the less educated men did better, although a few did not do so well as their better-educated compeers. The results are the same whether the data are examined in longitudinal or cross-sectional fashion. Prudential, which, unlike the companies discussed in Chapter IV, has done extensive research into its personnel practices, does not even consider formal education in the weighted application blank used in the selection of agents.

In another white-collar study, the results were in line with those already reported: Performance in 125 branch offices of a major New York bank, measured by turnover data and by the number of lost accounts per teller, was inversely associated with the educational achievements of these 500 workers.[7] The branches with the worst performance records were those in

---

[6] J. R. Milavsky, formerly of the Prudential Insurance Company, in communications to the author.

[7] Martin J. Gannon, "Employee Turnover and Productivity in a Branch Banking System," unpublished doctoral dissertation, Columbia University, 1969, written under the supervision of the author.

which a disproportionately (and significantly) high number of employees were attending educational programs after working hours! There was also evidence that performance was worst in precisely those branches in which, besides the educational achievements' being higher, the managers stressed education in consultations with tellers concerning their futures with the bank.

The fact that white-collar workers' job performances are more difficult to measure than those of blue-collar workers makes useful analysis in this area almost impossible. Salaried workers, for example, are not usually "docked" for the absences they incur whether they malinger, "go to the doctor," or attend to the myriad personal details of a folded, bent, and spindled society of forms, bureaus, licenses, and application blanks. Nor are formal records kept of the millions of hours spent on haircuts, apartment-hunting trips, brokerage-office visits, or headcolds by Americans whose salary checks presumably attest to their diligence and industry. The argument that these "breaks" are a factor in keeping employee morale high is rarely applied to the blue-collar worker who seeks to escape from the factory for no pleasure greater than his mother-in-law's funeral. The facts of life with respect to record-keeping guarantee that *any* criteria used by managers to screen employees can be *made* to work in the short run. And as my colleague and an authority on manpower problems, Professor Eli Ginzberg, has frequently observed, "The long run is, after all, only a series of short runs."

Professionals and Managers

Managerial and professional performance has long been a sticky issue in private enterprise, where handsome incomes are paid to highly placed leaders who preside over activities that are even more vulnerable to influences beyond corporate and managerial control than are those undertaken by insurance agents. It is a rare conference on "managing managers" or "managing scientists"—and there have been many in recent years—in which participants don't drink in frustrated fellowship at hotel bars where formal presentations on "management evaluation" are reviewed by skeptical "executive development" personnel. None of the executives we interviewed felt comfortable about his efforts in this much-plagued area, and none was able to provide any information useful in an appraisal of his experiences in the recruitment and development of managers and professionals.

Survey researchers at the Opinion Research Corporation of Princeton, New Jersey, however, have sought to identify some of the attitudes of engineers and scientists, including a few with administrative responsibilities, in an investigation sponsored by industry leaders concerned about the care and feeding of these high-priced personnel. Because employers had ranked the personnel ("A" or "B," according to their "value") from whom demographic and attitude data were solicited, it was possible to make at least an empirical excursion into the nettlesome issues involved.[8]

The personnel, nearly 620 of them, were employed by the nation's six largest manufacturers of heavy electrical equipment and appliances; the education-income nexus could thus be viewed in a comparative perspective, and logical inferences drawn concerning the hiring and salary policies of the six companies and the connections among company characteristics, personnel characteristics, and personnel satisfactions.

It may reasonably be assumed that the distributions of edu-

[8] The Opinion Research Corporation gave a duplicate deck of IBM cards containing the data used in the present study to the Roper Center at Williams College, Williamstown, Mass. We are indebted to the Director of the Roper Center, Dr. Phillip Hastings, for making these data available to us, and to the ORC for releasing the data for distribution by the Center.

cational achievements represented in each of the companies are indicators of that company's hiring policies. Engineers and scientists are more geographically mobile than most other occupational groups; moreover, each of the companies is large enough to recruit in a national labor market. Assuming, therefore, that the same types of men were available to all six companies, we can regard the fact that (for example) F had 62 Ph.D.'s among 96 employees whereas D had one Ph.D. in 100 to be the result of management choice. (See the cell numbers across the rows of Table V-1.)[9]

Table V-1 seems to show that income is tied to education more in some companies than in others: (a) The rank-order correlation (Tau Beta)[10] between education and income overall is quite high (.32) and is even higher in some companies; (b) the mean income for Ph.D's is uniformly much higher than the mean for groups with other educational achievements, in general and within each company; (c) the standard deviation of incomes around the mean is generally smaller for M.A.'s and Ph.D.'s than for people with less education, indicating that the income of those with less than an M.A. is determined by factors other than education, whereas M.A.'s or Ph.D.'s are paid primarily on the basis of their degrees.

The three companies that pay roughly the same average salaries appear to have strikingly different policies with respect to educational requirements. Company D either purposely hires people with modest educational achievements or largely ignores the factor of education in hiring and salary decisions.

[9] It is possible that the educational achievements of these personnel reflect company turnover experiences rather than hiring practices, but we cannot pursue this possibility with the data available.

[10] For a discussion of the Tau Beta statistic, see M. G. Kendall, *Rank Correlation Methods* (New York: Hafner, 1955) and Robert H. Somers, "A New Asymmetric Measure of Association for Ordinal Variables," *American Sociological Review*, XXVII, 6 (December, 1962). We are grateful to Dr. J. R. Milavsky, now of the National Broadcasting Corporation, for his statistical advice, and for the services of the Columbia Bureau of Applied Social Research.

TABLE V-1

MEAN ANNUAL SALARIES OF SCIENTISTS AND ENGINEERS AT SIX COMPANIES, BY EDUCATIONAL ACHIEVEMENT, 1958

Company[a]		Education						Tau β
		Less than Bachelor's Degree	B.A. or B.S.	Some Graduate Courses	M.A. or M.S.	Ph.D.	Total	
A	Mean	$7,750	$6,720	$7,500	$7,480	$9,390	$7,750	.45*
	S.D.	1,710	1,410	1,380	1,180	1,730	1,780	
	Number	(4)	(36)	(6)	(29)	(28)	(103)	
B	Mean	9,670	8,410	8,920	9,110	10,710	8,930	.24
	S.D.	1,530	2,040	2,190	1,560	1,680	2,040	
	Number	(3)	(59)	(12)	(19)	(14)	(107)	
C	Mean	8,000	8,440	7,500	8,310	11,030	9,170	.44*
	S.D.	2,000	2,270	1,050	1,570	1,450	2,190	
	Number	(3)	(32)	(6)	(26)	(32)	(99)	
D	Mean	9,450	9,340	9,440	10,880	16,000	9,580	.06
	S.D.	2,290	3,000	2,880	1,640	0	2,700	
	Number	(38)	(44)	(9)	(8)	(1)	(100)	
E	Mean	—	8,840	9,000	9,430	10,910	9,850	.35*
	S.D.	—	2,640	2,680	1,660	1,840	2,310	
	Number	(0)	(32)	(6)	(21)	(44)	(103)	
F	Mean	—	11,110	11,860	10,890	12,840	12,240	.28
	S.D.	—	2,420	2,730	2,170	2,330	2,450	
	Number	(0)	(9)	(7)	(18)	(62)	(96)	
Total	Mean	9,230	8,500	9,110	8,980	11,370	9,550	.32*
	S.D.	2,210	2,510	2,580	1,990	2,290	2,620	
	Number	(48)	(212)	(46)	(121)	(181)	(608)	

[a] Companies are listed in order of increasing mean annual salaries.
* Significant at .05 level. For an explanation of Tau β, see p. 96, n. 10.

Companies B and E distribute an almost identical amount of money to about the same number of men, but they do not similarly tie increments of income to increments of education; the relationship is stronger in E than in B. Finally, F, the company with by far the highest average salaries, has an apparently "moderate" tendency to tie rewards to degrees; within each group there is room for the "effect" of factors other than education.

Table V-2 reveals even more: it shows that, at least with respect to men with graduate degrees, management in these six companies tends to reward educational achievement rather than performance! Men with master's degrees who were designated by *management* as among 20 per cent of their scientists who were "relatively most valuable in terms of present performance and potential" were paid an average salary which was *$1,000 less* than that paid to Ph.D.'s, who were reportedly less valuable. Other data show that Ph.D.'s are paid substantially more even when they are younger and less experienced. Small wonder that these Ph.D.'s were a happy lot!

The data do not support the blanket inference that employers always reward educational achievement more than performance, but they afford presumptive evidence that this is the case. It is entirely likely that the numerous discrepancies between the evaluations and incomes earned by the subjects in the Opinion Research Corporation's survey are artifacts of the initial salary differentials which reflect different educational achievements. These differentials are easily maintained when subsequent salary increases are clustered in such a way as to reduce the likelihood that personnel will make "coercive comparisons" among themselves. In these six companies, at least, it appears that some less educated men earn through *performance* salaries that men with Ph.D.'s are given for their degrees.

A thorough search of the published literature on turnover and absenteeism in industry revealed that the matter of education is rarely considered among the factors linked to these

TABLE V-2

MEAN ANNUAL SALARIES OF SCIENTISTS AND ENGINEERS AT SIX COMPANIES, BY MANAGEMENT EVALUATION AND EDUCATION, 1958

Management Evaluation	Education						Tau β
	Less than Bachelor's Degree	B.A. or B.S.	Some Graduate Courses	M.A. or M.S.	Ph.D.	Total	
Ordinary							
Mean	$7,780	$7,500	$7,840	$8,270	$10,850	$8,460	.41*
S.D.	1,550	1,720	1,570	1,590	2,060	2,200	
Number	(27)	(128)	(25)	(66)	(71)	(317)	
Valuable							
Mean	11,100	10,020	10,620	9,840	11,710	10,750	.17
S.D.	1,370	2,710	2,770	2,090	2,370	2,520	
Number	(21)	(84)	(21)	(55)	(110)	(291)	
Total							
Mean	9,230	8,500	9,110	8,980	11,370	9,550	.32*
S.D.	2,210	2,510	2,580	1,990	2,290	2,620	
Number	(48)	(212)	(46)	(121)	(181)	(608)	

* Significant at the .05 level.

often-costly organizational problems. We reviewed hundreds of these studies and conclude, as did Gaudet, that in

> . . . seeking to learn the relation of turnover to education, level of skill, and marital status we find many general statements which are valueless, or worse, for decision-making.[11]

In those few studies in which the present interests can be pursued, the results are entirely in line with those presented. Thus a researcher and two executives examined the records of employees of the Bausch and Lomb Optical Company for a period after World War II, during which recruiting and training costs were "repaid" when an employee had worked for nine months. When they compared 27 employees who had remained on the jobs for nine months with those who had left within three months,

> . . . the results . . . show quite conclusively that, at the time of employment, employees who stay at least nine months on the job and [more] have had less formal education, are more frequently married, and have more dependents than employees who leave the job prior to three months.[12]

A few years later the Bureau of Labor Statistics examined the job changes of 1,700 apprentice and foreman tool and die workers in 300 plants located in two labor markets and reported a high positive correlation between years of formal education achieved and average number of job changes.[13]

And, in a study conducted at American Airlines of 2,015 "new hires" in all types of position, researchers concluded that there were no significant differences with respect to edu-

[11] F. J. Gaudet, "Labor Turnover: Calculation and Cost," *AMA Research Study No. 39* (New York: American Management Association, 1960), p. 79.
[12] Joseph Tiffin, "The Analysis of Personnel Data in Relation to Turnover on a Factory Job," *Journal of Applied Psychology*, XXXI (1947), 616.
[13] "The Mobility of Tool and Die Workers, 1940–1951," *Bulletin 1120, Bureau of Labor Statistics* (Washington: U.S. Department of Labor, 1952).

cation achieved between those who stayed and those who left.[14] Approximately the same results were reported in a comparison of the turnover rates of high-school and non-high-school graduates among 1,900 electronics technicians. Where 22 per cent of the non-high-school graduates had changed jobs, the figure for graduates was 25 per cent.[15]

Conclusion

The data in this chapter do not prove that educational requirements are bad; they do, however, reinforce doubts about whether the benefits that managers apparently believe accompany educational credentials do in fact materialize.

"But employers don't look for specific performance when they hire better-educated workers," some may argue. When they do, it is because they do not have evidence about the performance of the less educated workers who come to their personnel offices through contacts and references. Managers are concerned with generalized ability, and they believe that this can be ascertained through educational achievement.

Unfortunately, the data to test this hypothesis are not available. Some *pieces* of relevant evidence, however, suggest that the selection process is not so easily described. Professor Gary Becker (with an almost opposite purpose) sought to determine whether the individual returns on marginal investments in education are explained by the fact that higher-paid, better-educated workers are more able—i.e., more intelligent, and from backgrounds that make them more valuable to employers. His findings might embarrass an educator; they show that although there *is* a positive association between ability and educational

---

[14] Irwin W. Krantz, "Controlling Quick Turnover," *Personnel*, XXXI (1955), 514–20.

[15] James J. Treives, "Mobility of Electronics Technicians," *Monthly Labor Review*, LXXVII (1954), 263–66.

TABLE V-3

PROBABILITY OF ENTERING COLLEGE,
BY ABILITY AND SOCIOECONOMIC STATUS[a]

Ability Quarter	Socioeconomic Quarter			
	Low 1	2	3	High 4
Males				
Low 1	.06	.12	.13	.26
2	.13	.15	.29	.36
3	.25	.34	.45	.65
High 4	.48	.70	.73	.87
Females				
Low 1	.07	.07	.05	.20
2	.08	.09	.20	.33
3	.18	.23	.36	.55
High 4	.34	.67	.67	.82

[a] The samples from which these probabilities were calculated were high-school juniors in 1960.
SOURCE: Flanagan and Cooley, *op. cit.*, p. 95.

achievement, the latter accounts for *much* more of the variance in earnings. Although each of the studies he considers is deficient in one or more of the particulars of research design, the cumulative weight of the evidence, as he correctly points out, is impressive indeed.[16] "Consequently," he writes, "it may be concluded that, even after adjustment for differential ability, the private rate of return to a typical white male college graduate would be considerable, say, certainly more than 10 per cent."[17]

Becker's results should not surprise informed Americans, so frequently reminded that 15 to 20 per cent of all high-school students who are intellectually capable of going on to and completing an undergraduate program do not do so.[18] Table V-3 was developed by Project Talent to show the

[16] See Gary Becker, *Human Capital* (New York: Columbia University Press), 1964, p. 88.
[17] *Ibid.*, p. 88.
[18] Lyndon Baines Johnson, *State of the Union Address*, January 1968.

cross-influences of "socioeconomic status" and ability on the
probability of entering college. In every case, the probabilities
increase with *both* status and ability: The "ability score facili-
tates college entrance to a considerably greater degree than
does socioeconomic level."[19] For example, 70 per cent of the
males in the highest ability, second-socioeconomic quarter go
to college, compared to 36 per cent of the highest status,
second-quarter ability group. Thus students from lower socioeconomic classes, especially those with ability, have some
mobility, but this seems to be outweighed by the greater
probability that *all* ability groups among the high-status
groups will go on to college.

Again, Becker's findings on the returns from education and
ability do not disprove the greater value of an educated
worker over a less educated worker. Perhaps another researcher will be able to demonstrate that the credentialling
process has somewhat more measurable benefits than have
been uncovered in this study.

It is possible that there *are* benefits, and efforts to prove this
point may betray a misguided empiricism on the part of researchers. But the faith of some in the benefits of education is
perhaps no more valid than others' faith in the admittedly narrow issue of economic benefit. And one may well be skeptical,
if not cynical, about how much *real* education can be utilized
by most industrial organizations. Meanwhile, the contention
that people are changed as a function of their education and
thus can change the world gains at least as much horrifying as
gratifying support from history. One should note that there
are as many distinguished scholars advising the Department of
State on Vietnam as there are among critics of that department,
and that crackpot realism is no less prevalent among Ph.D.'s
than among less educated members of advisory staffs in military

[19] John C. Flanagan and William W. Cooley, *Project Talent: One-Year
Follow-Up Studies* (Pittsburgh: School of Education, University of
Pittsburgh, 1966), p. 95.

and other governmental units. To argue that well-educated people will automatically boost efficiency, improve organizations, and so on may be to misunderstand in a fundamental way the nature of American education, which functions to an important, indeed depressing, extent as a licensing agency.

A search of the considerable literature on productivity, absenteeism, and turnover has yielded little concrete evidence of a positive relationship between workers' educational achievements and their performance records in many work settings in the private sector. While psychologists, sociologists, and other professional students of behavior have attended to the problem of worker performance, these students, like business researchers, tend to contemplate the more esoteric variables with their complex theories. The literature is replete with contingency tables, regression equations, and "sociometric" diagrams that trace in embarrassing detail the relationships between the "sentiments," "activities," and "interactions" of workers and the "orientations" of supervisors, on the one hand, and the work accomplishments, especially of "work groups," on the other.

While these studies are not directly relevant to the present study, they have a strong indirect bearing upon it. Since many of them deal with the relationship between worker attitudes and productivity—when they deal with productivity at all—they provide us with clues to the dynamics of the education-production nexus. The present chapter has suggested that all this is more complex than might be inferred from the litany chanted by education's worshippers. It is thus useful to "go the next step" in this seemingly infinite regression to determine whether educational achievements are associated with the attitudes so frequently assumed to be predictors of productivity. The evidence, meanwhile, points to the need for a balanced perspective on the modest benefits that accrue to employers from using education as a screening device.

VI Educational Achievements and Job-related Attitudes

The observation that job-related attitudes may intervene between combinations of workers' demographic characteristics, including their educational backgrounds, and their job performance is based on an abundant technical literature. The precise role of attitudes, however, is not clearly delineated. The theoretical relevance of job-satisfaction studies, for example—the type of study that dominates this literature—is less than established.

Few Americans would argue that high levels of job dissatisfaction or other "negative" worker attitudes should be disregarded. But there is no way to determine how much dissatisfaction is too much, and the methods for determining the losses associated with "alienation" in the workplace are even more obscure.

Consider that worker turnover may result from dissatisfaction, but that turnover is part of "occupational mobility," and, as we have noted, turnover may simply be a marginal "corrective" of the process by which human resources are allocated. Such a corrective can take many forms, only some of which are accounted for in theoretical estimates of economic events.

During the course of the present study, one highly placed executive in a mammoth insurance company commented that "tender-minded academics" were "downright naive" in their concern about worker turnover and wellbeing. It was his "informed judgment" that clerical personnel

> . . . are easily trained for their jobs, that if they stayed on in larger numbers they would become wage problems—we'd have to keep raising them or end up fighting with them; they would form unions and who knows what the hell else. It's better to hire girls who are too well educated to *stay* happy with the jobs we assign them to do. That way they get out before it's too late.

To balance these and other more commonly expressed values related to labor mobility is not simple. Conversations with economists do not reassure one that a reasonable "benefit-cost analysis" of job dissatisfaction can be made in the present primitive state of their art. One complicating factor is that satisfied workers are sometimes more and sometimes less productive than their "alienated" workmates.[1]

It is likely that this fact, which has been noted by all who have addressed the problem, is an artifact of the methods of social-science investigators. One reviewer correctly concludes:

> . . . the amount of productivity on the job varies directly with the extent to which productive behavior is associated with satisfaction, and inversely with the extent to which nonproductive behavior is thus associated.[2]

[1] This is not the place to enter into a discussion of the tortured uses to which the concepts of "alienation" in general, and "worker alienation" in particular, have been put. It must suffice here to point out that the terms are abused if we are to understand that the user believes he is fingering the Marxist rosary. For three urbane discussions by one who is bothered by the unfortunate history of the concept as Marx employed it, see Daniel Bell, "The Meaning of Work," *New York Review of Books*, October 22, 1964, pp. 21–23; "The Rediscovery of Alienation: Some Notes Along the Quest for the Historical Marx," *Journal of Philosophy*, LVI (1959), 933–52; and "Work and Its Discontents," *The End of Ideology* (Glencoe: Free Press, 1960), Chapter 11.

[2] Raymond A. Katzell, "Personal Values, Job Satisfaction and Job Behavior," in Henry Borow, ed., *Man in a World at Work* (Boston: Houghton Mifflin, 1964), p. 356. See also Victor Vroom, *Work and Motivation* (New York, Wiley, 1964), pp. 262–64.

This formulation, he notes, "accommodates equally well findings of positive correlations, negative correlations, and zero correlations between the two types of variables."[3] The upshot is that the researcher must determine whether productivity itself is a source of satisfaction in order that a study of satisfaction and productivity can precipitate meaningful findings on the "utility" of efforts to heighten worker satisfaction. Until investigations are designed accordingly, the anomalies in the reports in this troublesome area must not be gainsaid.

For present purposes, it is conceded that job attitudes are not the clearest of scientific variables for theory construction. While there may well be an element of efficiency accruing to managers from their efforts to improve morale, the issue is by no means a dead one.[4] Perhaps more to the point than the incomplete evidence on the beneficial effects of morale among workers is the belief that, in an affluent society, a satisfied work force is to be preferred to a dissatisfied one, productivity, the "threat" of unions, and other questions quite aside.

Education and Job Satisfaction

On the score of job satisfaction, the evidence is somewhat more conclusive, if survey studies of worker attitudes are to be taken at face value.[5] From 1934 to 1963, employers have

[3] Katzell, op. cit., p. 356.

[4] For a cogent discussion of the findings when such efforts are made from the point of view of an economist concerned with extensions of theories of the firm, see Harvey Leibenstein, "Allocative Efficiency vs. 'X-Efficiency'," American Economic Review, LVI (1966), 392–415.

[5] Daniel Bell argues that such attitudes are useless for most purposes, for they are expressed by people with no realistic alternatives to the meaningless work they describe in response to the probes of social-science head-counters. See his remarks in a WBAI roundtable on "The Meaning of Work," summarized by Robert B. Cooney, "Democracy in the Work Place," American Federationist, LXIX (1962), 11.

cooperated with researchers who have produced no fewer than 450 percentage counts. The fact that "the median has fluctuated between 12- and 13-per cent dissatisfied for the past decade"[6] has not slowed or diminished the efforts of social scientists, nor has it stopped managers from seeking to document the malaise in their plants and offices or caused them to cut budgets for elaborate morale-building programs, complete with high-priced human-relations consultants, "sensitivity" trainers, and such exotic management gimmicks as "managerial grids."

Some—a small fraction—of these studies contain sufficient information to permit a review of the linkages between workers' educational achievements and the attitudes toward work that supposedly influence their work behavior. The following section points up once again the depressing fact that our faith in education gains little support from the social scientists.

Worker Satisfaction

Next to the findings that fewer than a quarter of all American workers are "dissatisfied" with their work, the survey result reported most frequently is that job satisfaction increases with job level. This finding is also consistently reported in other industrial nations, although the over-all percentage differences in satisfaction among countries are considerable.[7] Thus, social scientists document the association of personal expectations

---

[6] H. Alan Robinson, Ralph P. Connors, and Ann H. Robinson, "Job Satisfaction Researches of 1963," *Personnel and Guidance Journal*, XLIII (1964), 36. This is the 22nd in a continuing series, the bibliographical notations for which are given in this 1964 report.

[7] See Alex Inkeles, "Industrial Man: The Relation of Status to Experience, Perception and Value," *American Journal of Sociology*, LXVI (1960), 1-31.

For American data, see F. Herzberg, B. Mausner, and R. O. Petersonn, *Job Attitudes: Review of Research and Opinion* (Pittsburgh: Psychological Service of Pittsburgh, 1947), p. 20; and Vroom, *op. cit.*, pp. 129-32.

with job attitudes;[8] workers who hold high-level jobs and whose occupational expectations have therefore been more nearly fulfilled are more likely to be satisfied than those with frustrated job dreams.

These findings point to the strong likeihood that worker expectations are the most promising subject of research with respect to job attitudes. And it requires little imagination to hypothesize that workers' educational backgrounds may be a major determinant of their occupational expectations and hence of their satisfactions. Educational achievements can predictably be associated with higher job expectations; consequently, attitudes toward work would be more favorable among better-educated workers as their occupational skills increase.

Unfortunately, this hypothesis is not examined even in studies in which investigators troubled to collect information on workers' educational backgrounds. There is a tendency, perhaps the result of a trained incapacity to confront the obvious in favor of status-enhancing scientism, to cross-tabulate attitudes with such exotic variables as ego involvement rather than with more commonplace demographic characteristics. To judge from the two dozen studies that do afford an opportunity to examine all or parts of the hypothesis, it is probably valid.

In one of the early and most widely cited studies of workers' satisfaction, Dr. Nancy Morse attributed the bulk of the observed differences between satisfied and dissatisfied clerical employees to variations in the supervisory styles to which these 742 low- and middle-skill-level white-collar personnel were exposed. A close examination of the data, however, reveals that the differences in satisfactions between the less and better-educated workers in each of several skill groups were as great as or greater than the differences among workers

---

[8] Katzell, *op. cit.*, p. 263.

broken down according to their supervisors on two of three dimensions of satisfaction employed in the study. With regard to the third dimension, the better-educated were "more satisfied," a reversal the author notes but does not fully explain, in a study that stresses the significance of supervisory "styles" for worker satisfaction.[9]

In a 1957 review, Professors Herzberg, Mausner, and Peterson located 13 relevant studies, and they reported that

> . . . five show no difference in job attitudes among workers differing in education; three show an increase in morale with increased education; another five show that the higher these workers' educational level, the lower their morale . . . . The three studies showing increased morale with education are in no case very conclusive . . . ; [they] were carried out either with groups having a restricted range of education, or with groups in unusual circumstances [e.g., retarded workers].[10]

A somewhat more specific test of the hypothesis was made in an investigation which concluded that the best-paid workers, who presumably were not doing tedious work and had lower educational achievements, were the employees with the highest levels of job satisfaction.[11] Herzberg's review indicates that this is indeed the case; the inverse relationship between educational achievement and work satisfaction in a given job category is reduced, *though not eliminated*, as the attitudes of successively older workers are examined.

Herzberg's conclusion is in basic accord with more general formulations in his field. Discussion in psychological circles in recent years posits a need to reduce dissonance among "cog-

[9] Nancy Morse, *Satisfaction in the White Collar Job* (Ann Arbor, University of Michigan, Institute for Social Research, Survey Research Center, 1953). Efforts to recover the original data from the Survey Research Center and from Dr. Morse were not successful.

[10] Herzberg *et al.*, *op. cit.*, pp. 15–16.

[11] Richard Centers and Hadley Cantril, "Income Satisfaction and Income Aspiration," *Journal of Abnormal and Social Psychology*, XLI (1956), 64–69.

nitions" and indicates that age, as well as educational achievement, should influence peoples' attitudes toward their work. Discrepancies between what people believe to be true and what they believe *should* be true, it is argued, are painful, and people seek to reduce that pain by changing their beliefs, or by elaborating them, so that beliefs and realities seem to become consistent.[12] Thus, as better-educated workers with lower-level jobs get older, they find various rationalizations that explain away the continuing discrepancy between their aspirations and rewards.

That an appropriately modified hypothesis has merit seems to be a justifiable inference drawn from a brace of investigations. Howard Vollmer and Jack Kinney report unambiguous results in a study of more than 2,220 civilians employed by the Army's Ordnance Corps in the 1950's. The per cent of these employees "satisfied" and "highly satisfied" goes down, and the per cent dissatisfied goes up, as educational achievements go up from grammar school, through high school, and up to college. The hypothesis that the older, well-educated workers may reduce "cognitive dissonance" by reappraising their jobs is perhaps borne out by the authors' finding that "education is more highly related to job satisfaction than is age, although both seem to have a definite relation to the degree of job satisfaction."[13]

The authors are careful to specify that "when management wishes to develop people in certain positions in the light of their long-range potentialities, [the] preference for younger and higher educated applicants may be justified." This observation, while perhaps appropriate in a study that is substantially subversive of managers' theories about educated workers, did not win support in the previous chapter, and

---

[12] Leon A. Festinger, *A Theory of Cognitive Dissonance* (Evanston, Ill.: Row, Peterson, 1957).

[13] Howard M. Vollmer and Jack A. Kinney, "Age, Education and Job Satisfaction," *Personnel*, XXXII (1955), 38–43.

there are some grounds for believing that many better-educated workers gain "real" promotions by interfirm rather than intrafirm mobility.

The data on the relationships between educational achievement and occupational accomplishment suggest a further refinement of the earlier hypothesis. One might expect, from the studies reviewed, that relationships between educational achievement, opportunities for advancement (real or perceived), and job attitudes parallel those bearing on education, occupational achievement, and attitudes. Once again, the work of previous researchers is less than fully revealing; their preoccupation with complex psychological and sociological constructs appears to get in the way of what are presumably more pedestrian, although they may be more productive, lines of inquiry.

It is likely that if the investigators traced their way back from "achievement motives," for example, they would be able to give such abstractions higher orders of specificity. It should be apparent that if "ego involvement" is a prerequisite to job satisfaction in a particular job setting, it would be useful to know what *kinds* of people are likely to experience such involvement, and what kinds of conditions encourage or reinforce it.

Employers, we may be sure, can more easily screen applicants than they can *shape* them; managers, after all, do not typically operate in a labor market in which they have *no* choice in the matter. And the tendency to screen out the less educated personnel may, in fact, have the effect of constraining choice on emprically questionable grounds. It is not insignificant that dissatisfaction is from two to four times greater among the better- than the less educated group in the Vollmer-Kinney study, while there is a regular difference of 10 percentage points between the satisfied and the highly satisfied among the better-educated subjects.

Two IBM researchers studied the educational credentials

and work satisfaction of 727 employees, half of the first-level supervisory personnel, in a large American corporation in the context of the so-called reference groups of these personnel. It was their hypothesis, in the curious language of their otherwise lucid report, that

. . . college education or lack thereof constitutes a key input in the individual's self-evaluation. This self-evaluation in turn leads to expectations regarding salary opportunities which in turn affect satisfactions with present salary conditions. As a consequence, we would expect that having attended college would negatively affect satisfaction with pay since, for any given pay level, the college-trained person will be further away from the set of expectations he holds for himself. Further, if these expectations are held constant, then the difference between the college-educated and the non-college-educated should disappear because this would also partially control for reference groups, self-concept, and aspiration level.[14]

In addition to age and skill level, their analysis took into account the respondents' perceptions of getting comparable jobs elsewhere and of earning more money on their present jobs.

The findings were that satisfaction goes down with increasing education and that, although optimistic "external" expectations reduced the magnitude of the observed relationship, the differences by educational achievement remained greater than would be likely by chance. The differences nearly disappeared when satisfactions with present pay were compared in juxtaposition with the duties and responsibilities of the respondents, but the finding that "higher education in [this] sample is associated with relative dissatisfaction with pay" was not vitiated when the respondents' age and skill level were held constant.[15]

In the study of 550 bank employees reported in Chapter V,

[14] S. M. Klein and J. R. Maher, "Education Level and Satisfaction with Pay," *Personnel Psychology*, XIX (1962), 198.
[15] *Ibid.*, p. 204.

similar patterns emerged. When "better" and "less" educated tellers were compared, the former were overrepresented among those critical of management, and the latter were slightly overrepresented among those who were favorably disposed toward a long series of management practices considered in the study.

Some of the bank's managers tended also to emphasize the significance of educational achievement for promotions within the organization. One of the results of this practice—which is sometimes used by these managers to avoid acknowledging their impotence with respect to promotion policy, and sometimes to discourage valued employees from seeking transfers that would facilitate their own but not the manager's organizational career—is that approximately 150 of these tellers attended school after working hours. The modest educational differences were sharpened appreciably when these tellers' attitudes were compared to those of non-attenders. Indeed, the two most powerful predictors of dissatisfaction were the emphasis managers placed on education for promotion and the factor of attendance in after-hour educational programs, findings that parallel the results with respect to performance, reported earlier.

Dr. Edward M. Lehman, of Cornell University's Medical Center, examined the mobility patterns and satisfactions of men in practically every position within a regional affiliate of a large nationwide utilities industry.[16] His findings are altogether consistent with the theme in the present analysis. His sample included college and non-college men, and he reasoned that their "promotion satisfactions" could be interpreted only by examining their promotion experiences together with their educational backgrounds. After establishing the fact that the better-educated group had greater "initial opportunity," Lehman compared the satisfactions of more and less mobile men and

---

[16] Edward M. Lehman, "Mobility and Satisfaction in an Industrial Organization," unpublished Ph.D. dissertation, Columbia University, 1966.

found that although actual mobility experience is important in predicting promotion satisfaction, the prediction can be sharpened by considering initial opportunity. His findings are reported in Table VI-1.

TABLE VI-1

SATISFACTION WITH PROMOTIONS,
BY INITIAL OPPORTUNITY FOR MOBILITY AND ACTUAL MOBILITY

Initial Opportunity	Actual Mobility	% Satisfied	Number Satisfied
Low	Low	33.7	83
Low	Moderate	62.4	93
Low	High	76.2	42
High	Low	27.3	44
High	High	72.0	50

SOURCE: Lehman, op. cit., p. 79.

Lehman also reports a close association between his respondents' satisfaction with promotion and their satisfactions with other aspects of the job.

Fred Goldner also considered the satisfactions with their promotions of 337 managers employed by a large electronics manufacturer in 1963; his findings are entirely in line with Lehman's.[17] He divided his managers into groups according to their length of service with the company, and reports that satisfaction is inversely related to educational achievements among managers in all three of the groups so constructed. The data are presented in Table VI-2. The percentages in the table refer to the percentage of respondents whose answers to the question "Are you satisfied with your advancement?" were below the mean of 7.5, which was used as the break-point for determining high and low satisfactions on a scale from 0 to 10.

---

[17] Fred Goldner, "Organizations in Motion," research in progress on management as a work force, Columbia University Graduate School of Business. Personal communication to the author.

TABLE VI-2

PERCENTAGE OF MANAGERS REPORTING LOW SATISFACTION
WITH THEIR PROMOTIONS, BY YEARS OF COMPANY SERVICE
AND EDUCATION

Years of Company Service	Education		
	Not a College Graduate	College Graduate	Advanced Degree
7 or less	— (2)[a]	30 (44)	36 (22)
8–15	14 (29)	35 (101)	47 (43)
16 or more	36 (58)	45 (33)	— (5)
Total	28 (89)	35 (178)	43 (70)

[a] The numbers in parentheses represent the base on which percentages were calculated; per cents are not shown for small bases.

SOURCE: Goldner, *op. cit.*

Corollaries of Dissatisfaction

That some job dissatisfactions are of more than routine interest is strongly suggested by the limited data available relating education with turnover and with workers' mental health.

Professor Bullock reports, in a study of 70 former employees and 100 present clerical employees of an Ohio company, that former employees had more job experience, were older, and had more formal education than present employees. The average scores of the two groups on scales purportedly measuring their satisfactions were also significantly different.[18] Form and Geschwender also discovered that there were statistically significant inverse relationships between the sat-

[18] Robert Bullock, *Social Factors Related to Job Satisfaction* (Columbus: Bureau of Business Research, College of Commerce and Administration, Ohio State University, 1952).

isfactions and turnover rates of better- and less educated workers.[19]

These findings corroborate those reported in one of the most widely cited studies of "the occupational plans of workers" by Yale's distinguished labor economist, Professor Lloyd Reynolds. He reported, in the early 1950's, that workers with a high-school education or better showed a markedly greater desire to change jobs. In some cases their responses, as Professor Reynolds points out, probably reflected a desire to escape from manual work altogether.[20] He writes, "Of those with more than 12 years of education, 36 per cent [in one sample] and 48 per cent [in a second] wanted to leave their present job. Of those with four years or less of education, on the other hand, only 13 per cent . . . and none [in the two worker samples, respectively] wanted to leave."[21]

The deplorable quality of research on turnover makes it impossible to pursue this issue further in the present study. It is perhaps remarkable to note, in this connection, that though turnover was frequently mentioned as a problem facing the personnel executives with whom interviews were conducted, none had compared the characteristics, including the educational achievements, of short- and long-service employees despite the fact that relevant personnel data were retained in personnel files for long periods.

When better-educated people do not enjoy consistency between their educational and occupational statuses, they may also be more interested in union activities. In a study of New York cab drivers, Al Nash identified the success of their union with the efforts of a group of drivers who had attended a

[19] William H. Form and James H. Geschwender, "Social Reference Basis of Job Satisfaction: The Case of Manual Workers," *American Sociological Review*, XXVII (1962), 228–37.

[20] Lloyd G. Reynolds, *The Structure of Labor Markets* (New York: Harper and Bros., 1951), p. 80.

[21] *Ibid.*, p. 81.

training program conducted in New York City by Cornell's
School of Industrial Relations. This group, which rated their
"self-esteem" higher than the non-attending groups, was also
disproportionately better educated than the more passive
group of drivers.[22] One implication of such findings is that
union leaders have better empirical reasons for concentrating
on educational achievement in their recruiting efforts than do
managers.

Finally, it would not be surprising, in light of the foregoing
analysis, if better-educated workers in a given job category in
fact suffered more than the frustration generated by the gap
between their occupational achievements and the expectations
to which their educational achievements may contribute. This
is implied in an interesting study, *Mental Health of the Industrial Worker*,[23] in which the sample was broken down by skill
levels according to official job titles, "clarified when necessary
by consultation with automotive 'insiders'; the worker's own
description of his duties, job operations, and training time required; and the rate of pay."[24] Mental-health scores were derived from six component indexes and two composite indexes
constructed from coded responses to a carefully structured interview. The coding process was validated by a comparison of
scores with clinical judgments of the interview material (for
40 cases) by "several experienced, highly qualified clinical
psychologists and psychiatrists." The level of agreement,[25]
especially as these things go, was remarkably high.

The over-all results do not confirm the expectations that
better-educated men in routine jobs exhibit poorer mental
health than do those with less education, possibly, as Kornhauser suggests, because the effects of education when skill

[22] Al Nash, "A Study of New York's Taxicab Union," unpublished
Master's Essay, Department of Sociology, Columbia University, 1967.

[23] Arthur Kornhauser, *Mental Health of the Industrial Worker* (New
York: Wiley, 1965).

[24] *Ibid.*, p. 56.

[25] *Ibid.*, p. 31.

level is held constant "are offset or overbalanced by *other* ways in which education relates to mental health."[26] Comparisons of school success did show a little support for the notion that "status inconsistency" can generate problems, although the support is shaky in that, while a relatively small proportion of the group in low-level jobs whose school success had been above average manifested good mental health, this group had relatively few respondents with poor mental health compared with those whose school accomplishments had been below average.

When Kornhauser undertook to perform a more refined analysis, however, the picture changed somewhat. Better-educated workers in lower skill-level jobs had lower "life satisfaction" and "self-esteem" scores, although the "personal morale" and "sociability" scores among the middle-aged and the younger middle-aged, respectively, were higher than among the less educated workers. While these tendencies are counter-balancing and thus tend to cancel out the effects of "inconsistency" between education and occupation,

> . . . the two particular mental health dimensions that do manifest the [incongruency hypothesis] relationship are precisely the ones that might be most expected to do so. Self-esteem and satisfaction with life can be presumed to depend to greater degree on vocational achievement in relation to aspirations than would feelings of social distrust (personal morale), social withdrawal, and other elements of mental health, which are more likely to derive from lifelong influences apart from the job.[27]

The relevant data are presented in Table VI-3, on the following page.

These findings can give precious little comfort to morale-conscious executives who might more easily improve the

---

[26] *Ibid.*, p. 136. Emphasis in original.
[27] *Ibid.*, p. 137.

TABLE VI-3

PERCENTAGE OF EDUCATIONAL GROUPS AT TWO
LOWEST OCCUPATIONAL LEVELS WHO HAVE HIGH SCORES
ON SELECTED MENTAL-HEALTH COMPONENTS

Mental-Health Components	Young		Middle-Aged		
	Some High School or Less	High-School Graduates	8th Grade or Less	Some High School	High-School Graduates
Life satisfaction	25	11	38	33	18
Self-esteem	18	11	22	14	12
Personal morale	25	21	19	32	59
Sociability	32	47	21	44	59
Number	(57)	(19)	(81)	(57)	(17)

SOURCE: Kornhauser, *op. cit.*, p. 137.

"human relations" climates and the "self-actualizing" potentials of their personnel by modifying their own attitudes toward educational credentials. It is no doubt a good deal easier to alter these attitudes than to manipulate the psyches of employees whose educations generate expectations well beyond those that the organization can fulfill.

The general line of analysis in this chapter was put to more refined tests in a revealing reinterpretation of data collected by the Roper organization. The fact that these particular materials have already provoked widespread interest among students of worker "alienation" and have even been the subject of one large-scale report[28] justifies the allocation of an entire chapter to their exploitation, the task of Chapter VII.

[28] Robert Blauner, *Alienation and Freedom* (Chicago: University of Chicago Press, 1964).

VII The Blue-Collar Worker: A Special Case

Several reasons have already been suggested for the seemingly perverse relationships between educational achievement and work performance. Contrary to popular belief, education does not always group people according to their abilities, especially the abilities to do specific jobs. This fact reflects, not only the great variations in standards among the nation's thousands of school systems and institutions of higher learning, but the parallel differences among the units within a system and even within a given school. In addition, there may be some truth in the adage that "you can't keep a good man down" in a society in which there are discrepancies between educators' and employers' definitions of a "good man."

Beyond the question of ability, however, lies the more subtle one of motivation, a question that can be tackled indirectly through an examination of the satisfactions of workers while their educational achievements and their job levels are held constant. The results help to explain why the oft-cited positive relationship between job level and work satisfaction is far from perfect.

We have already implied that Americans are influenced by the vulgarization of the argument that they have foregone incomes to complete their education. The popular culture plus experiences within the educational apparatus itself, with its implicitly or explicitly vocational aims, its placement personnel, guidance counselors, career-day programs, and employer interviews—all add independent weight to the widespread expectations among Americans that they deserve jobs that are interesting, that they will be promoted on the basis of abilities to which their diplomas and degrees give testimony, and that they will make money. "To get a better job, get a better education," reads the subway placard; "things are changing," says the disc jockey, "and so," he quickly adds, "finish your education to get a bigger piece of the action and a better job."

When their jobs are dull, when their chances of promotion are slim, when their salaries are dissappointingly low, then employees are dissatisfied, poorly motivated, and poorer employees; if they can, they change jobs. But if, over the years, they do not search out better jobs, or if family and other obligations limit their movement into more rewarding and gratifying work experiences, or if successive job changes have shown that their aspirations cannot be fulfilled, they begin to accommodate, to "settle in," to lower their aspirations, and to rationalize their circumstances; their dissatisfaction, though persistent, diminishes.

This argument is supported by data already presented. It is possible, however, to forge some of the links in the chain of reasoning through the detailed analysis of a special case—the blue-collar worker.

A "job satisfaction" study, conducted by the Roper organization for the editors of *Fortune* Magazine, provides information on the desire for promotion, the perceived chances for promotion, and the job satisfactions of 2,139 blue-collar respondents.[1] The survey was conducted among workers in 16 industries and, according to Elmo Roper and Robert Blauner, "Although not a random probability sample . . . [it was] 'a pretty carefully controlled quota sample,' and therefore representative of a population much larger than

---

[1] Data from this study were made available by the Roper Center at Williams College, Williamstown, Mass.; once again we are indebted to its director, Professor Phillip Hastings, and to his staff.

the 3,000 workers interviewed."[2] According to Elmo Roper and Associates, "Within the universe defined, the sample was so stratified as to contain the proper distribution of respondents by sex, geographic area, race, and age according to the Census of 1940,"[3] all of which is to say that the results, in their time, could probably be generalized to a substantial part of the blue-collar work force.

From the 3,000 workers originally interviewed, we removed the foremen and the women; our analysis is thus based on 2,139 males below the rank of foreman in 16 industries across the United States.[4]

Education and Skill

Our first analysis of the data consisted of a series of rank-order correlations[5] between each of 15 questions measuring satisfaction and the workers' background characteristics. The results showed that:

1. Education is indeed strongly associated with aspirations,

[2] Robert Blauner, *Alienation and Freedom* (Chicago: University of Chicago Press, 1964), in a citation from his correspondence with Mr. Roper, p. 16, note 11. Professor Blauner used these same "Roper data" in his book.

[3] Survey #58, *Fortune*, January, 1947.

[4] Since aspirations might reasonably be expected to be related to both educational achievement and job attitudes, 238 foremen were eliminated from the sample because they had reached the top of the blue-collar hierarchy, were more skilled, better educated, and had longer service than the larger group. Answers to such questions as "Does your job lead to promotion?" and questions dealing with aspiration to be foremen were uninterpretable when the respondents included both foremen and men of lesser rank. Women were also dropped because in an initial set of tabulations it became clear that the most interesting and crucial patterns in the results were substantially blurred by their inclusion. Women, particularly low earners, often work to supplement their husband's income and regard occupational issues as less salient than other issues facing them, a fact that argued for their exclusion.

[5] In this and later analyses of rank correlation the Tau Beta statistic was used. For a discussion of this statistic, see p. 96, *n*. 10.

whether those aspirations are measured in terms of a desire to be foreman or, alternatively, to be a union official;

2. Although education is weakly and sometimes insignificantly (though inversely) associated with work satisfactions, the "effects" of education are more intense among higher-aspiring workers.

3. Skill levels consistently "predicted" satisfactions and dissatisfactions. People with low-skill jobs were dissatisfied; the percentage satisfied increased in each category of increasing skill.[6]

The patterns of response to the question, "Is [your job] too simple to bring out your best abilities, or not?" are perhaps the most interesting and relevant to the present analysis. The question refers specifically to a dimension of work experiences that would involve a consideration of educational background.

The association between answers to this question and to others indicates that it can legitimately be construed as bearing upon dissatisfactions and satisfactions of workers. In survey research it is not uncommon to validate a question by comparing the responses it evokes with other seemingly independent measures. Judged by this standard, the validity, so-called, of this question is high. Respondents who stated that their jobs were too simple to utilize their abilities tended also to say that their jobs "do not enable them to try their own ideas," that their jobs permitted them "to do their work, and keep [their] minds on other things," and that they did not find their jobs "nearly always" or "mostly" interesting. They tended to reject the proposition that their "jobs would lead to promotion if done well." Moreover, these answers were most

[6] The data provided no direct information on skill level. In his book-length treatment of worker "alienation," based on these same data, Professor Robert Blauner assigned skill levels to the respondents in accordance with the number of months of training or experience they reported to be necessary to enable them to handle the jobs they held at the time of the survey. This procedure has been followed in the present study. Thus "skill level," the term used here, is really an indirect measure of job complexity.

strongly linked to one another among those with more education working in lower-skill jobs. In light of these patterns in the responses to the question of whether the job was too simple for their abilities, it has been used as an all-purpose measure of job satisfaction; those who regard their jobs as "too simple" are dissatisfied.

Table VII-1 shows a dramatic correlation between education and satisfaction. Reading across, we see that dissatisfaction, the feeling that the job is too simple for the worker's abilities, decreases with increased skill required except among those with less than a grade-school education. In the exceptional case, however, the numbers are too small for meaningful comparison.

Reading down, dissatisfaction increases with increased education among all but those in jobs requiring the most skill. The over-all rank correlation between dissatisfaction and skill is substantially increased for those with high-school or college education. (See the column on the far right.) This means that dissatisfaction is even more closely tied to skill level among better-educated employees than it is for the group as a whole.

Because of the empirical importance of skill for satisfaction, and because the logic of the argument calls for the comparison of better-educated with less educated men doing approximately similar jobs, the men were divided into four categories (Table VII-2);[7] these categories are descriptive of workers' "status inconsistency" because they indicate whether a man's skill level is in line with his educational level.

The four resulting combinations of education-plus-skill can be located on a continuum describing the degree of "fit" between education and job; this two-dimensional characteristic of workers closely approximates an accurate index of "status

---

[7] This procedure has the additional virtue that it creates categories large enough to permit further subdivisions according to age, length of service, and other characteristics.

TABLE VII-1

PERCENTAGE OF BLUE-COLLAR WORKERS DISSATISFIED, BY EDUCATION AND SKILL

Education	Skill (in training time required for job)					
	Less than 1 Month	1–3 Months	3–24 Months	More than 2 Years	Total	Tau β
None	20 (15)[a]	0 (4)	57 (7)	38 (8)	29 (34)	−.21
1–8 years	38 (275)	33 (116)	17 (217)	15 (219)	26 (827)	.20*
9–12 years	58 (216)	39 (107)	28 (279)	16 (271)	33 (873)	.31**
More than 12 years	50 (10)	75 (4)	29 (21)	16 (31)	29 (66)	.30
Total	46 (516)	36 (231)	23 (524)	16 (529)		.24**[b]
Tau β	−.20	−.11	−.10	.01	−.07[c]	

[a] The numbers in parentheses represent the base on which percentages were calculated.
[b] Tau β between dissatisfaction and skill.
[c] Tau β between dissatisfaction and education.
* Significant at the .05 level.
** Significant at the .01 level.

TABLE VII-2
EDUCATION AND SKILL COMBINED TO FORM A
STATUS-INCONSISTENCY VARIABLE

| Education (in years) | Skill (months of training time required for job) | |
	High (3 or more)	Low (Less than 3)
Low (0–8)	Inconsistent Most satisfaction (451)[a]	Consistent 3d most satisfaction (410)
High (9 or more)	Consistent 2d most satisfaction (602)	Inconsistent Least satisfaction (337)

[a] The number of men in the status-inconsistency category.

inconsistency"; that is, the relative discrepancy between a man's educational and occupational achievement.[8]

Accordingly, workers with high-skill jobs and comparatively low educational achievements would consider themselves fortunate and theoretically would be the most content because they enjoy rewards that are "inconsistently" high given their educational status. The next most content group would be the one in which work rewards match (in accordance with prevailing norms) educational achievement. People in low-skilled jobs and with low educational achievements would be less happy than those in the first two groups simply because their rewards are low; the *most* dissatisfied, however,

[8] The concept of "status inconsistency" or "status incongruence" is by no means new; indeed, the notion is often invoked in a variety of guises in efforts to understand social systems, large and small. See, for example, Gerhard Lenski, "Status Crystalization: A Non-Vertical Dimension of Social Status," *American Sociological Review*, XIX (1954,) 405–13. The idea in part is that social status has a number of hierarchical dimensions, that individuals occupy positions on each of these hierarchies, that social norms define the ranking of positions on each of these hierarchies, and that people whose position on one dimension is "incongruent" with their position on another suffer various social and psychological strains. The concept has been questioned both methodologically and theoretically, but it serves as a convenient shorthand for the two variables we are combining here.

would be those whose low-skilled jobs provide returns below those perceived to be due people with relatively *high* educational achievements, and whose rewards are "inconsistently" low in the light of their education. Once again, the concept of status inconsistency in the present context refers to the identity or discrepancy between the rewards a person's status in a social setting could be expected to earn him (according to prevailing standards), on the one hand, and the rewards he actually receives, on the other. The results of the analysis throughout this chapter are consistent with this formulation in almost every particular.[9]

Aspirations and Expectations

The explanation of the fact that men with more education are more dissatisfied with low-skilled jobs than are those with less education appears to lie in expectations: Better-educated men expect to do better.

Table VII-3 shows not only that better-educated men want to be foremen, but that more of these workers consider the prospect likely. That their estimates are realistic may be inferred from the fact that better-educated men do have a better chance: Foremen, excluded from our study, were indeed better educated. And better-educated men see more likelihood of being promoted above the foreman's level. They are also more likely to say that their "job leads to promotion" in general.

[9] The use of the concept "status consistency" borrows the very assumptions of the education-employment nexus this study undertook to explore. If the nature of the link between education and job level is to be seriously questioned, as argued in this book, then there is no educational level that is *per se* "consistent" with any particular skill level. But the conventional wisdom on the relationship of rewards to education and the linkage of income differences to occupational differences has been stamped into the wax of culture and psyche; to question the value of these rigidities and prescriptions, one must first demonstrate their impact.

TABLE VII-3

PERCENTAGE OF BLUE-COLLAR WORKERS DISSATISFIED[a], BY STATUS
INCONSISTENCY AND PERCEIVED LIKELIHOOD OF BECOMING A FOREMAN

Perceived Likelihood of Becoming a Foreman[b]	Status Inconsistency					
	Low Ed– High Skill	High Ed– High Skill	Low Ed– Low Skill	High Ed– Low Skill	Total	Tau β
Likely	8 (60)[c]	16 (147)	18 (28)	40 (58)	19 (293)	.23
Unlikely	24 (74)	31 (108)	43 (79)	65 (79)	40 (340)	.31*

[a] In this and subsequent tables, those who are classified as dissatisfied are those who consider their job too simple for their abilities.

[b] This question was asked only of those answering affirmatively when asked whether they would like to be a foreman.

[c] The numbers in parentheses represent the base on which percentages were calculated.

* Significant at the .05 level.

When these aspirations are not satisfied, when their desire to be promoted seems likely to be disappointed, all of these workers are more dissatisfied with their jobs, but those with relatively more education and less skill are especially disaffected; the proportion who are dissatisfied increases by 25 per cent. Even among the relatively happy skilled men with little education, dissatisfaction triples, from 8 to 24 per cent, when they think it unlikely that they will rise to foremen.

Employers' notions about the desirability of hiring better-educated people in order to have a pool of promotable people, therefore, might well help generate discontent among better-educated, aspiring workers in low-skilled jobs, and particularly in shops and factories in which these workers perceive comparatively little chance of being promoted.

Furthermore, the predictions made in connection with "status inconsistency" are confirmed here as they are throughout the analysis: dissatisfaction increases uniformly, from the relatively contented man in a high-skill job despite low education (in the far left column), through the quite discontented man in a low-skill job. This stepwise pattern can be seen even among those who expect their aspirations to become foremen to be fulfilled. Forty per cent of the better-educated men in the lowest skilled jobs who think they *will* become foremen are unhappy.[10]

The impact of frustrated expectations on dissatisfaction is exactly the same when promotion possibilities are tapped by two other questions: "What are your chances of being promoted to a job above the foreman's level?" and "Does your job lead to promotion?" The pattern of the results was identical to that found in Table VII-3. Even the percentages were similar.[11]

Once again, the effect of status inconsistency is mitigated, but not eliminated, by (perceived) opportunities for promotion. Dissatisfactions which are born of the feeling that a job is too simple for one's abilities and which grow with increasing education among less skilled workers are only somewhat modified by opportunities for organizational advancement.

Employers who assert that better-educated workers are only temporarily "misplaced" in their firm, that they plan to promote these men, and that eventual promotion will mitigate the effects of the underutilization of educated manpower may well be correct. The tables indicate, however, that some skepticism is justified; even when these workers perceive that they will have the opportunity to advance, their dissatisfactions are relatively high. And there simply cannot be enough positions as foremen in industry to accommodate all who want them. The fact that foremen in American industry increasingly come from the ranks of college graduates makes the matter even more problematical.

[10] All of these men want to be foremen and think they will make it, yet a substantial minority see even this job as too simple. The contrast with the less educated men with high skills is particularly striking.

[11] Although differences between "aspirers" and "nonaspirers" were never more than four percentage points, they were always in the predicted direction.

TABLE VII-4

PERCENTAGE OF BLUE-COLLAR WORKERS DISSATISFIED, BY
STATUS INCONSISTENCY AND YEARS OF COMPANY SERVICE

Years of Company Service	Status Inconsistency					
	Low Ed– High Skill	High Ed– High Skill	Low Ed– Low Skill	High Ed– Low Skill	Total	Tau β
Less than 2	27 (85)a	17 (186)	44 (152)	54 (169)	36 (592)	.32**
2–5	19 (73)	27 (132)	39 (78)	48 (61)	31 (344)	.20
More than 5	14 (292)	23 (283)	27 (180)	51 (107)	24 (862)	.23*

a The numbers in parentheses represent the base on which percentages
were calculated.
* Significant at the .05 level.
** Significant at the .01 level.

Settling for Less

With dissatisfactions of this magnitude, with the expanded
opportunities for switching jobs in the "tight labor market"
of 1947, the year the study took place, we can conclude that
many of the most dissatisfied workers left for other jobs. The
studies described in Chapter V indicated that better-educated
men have greater tendencies to leave their jobs. Unfortunately, information on turnover for the men in the Roper survey is not available, but what may be assumed to be the
indirect effects of turnover are visible in the data.

Table VII-4 squares well with the hypothesis that dissatisfied workers leave their jobs. Except for those with consistently high education and skill, dissatisfaction is greater
among those with short service.

As men see their hopes still unrealized as they grow older,

TABLE VII-5

PERCENTAGE OF BLUE-COLLAR WORKERS DISSATISFIED,
BY STATUS INCONSISTENCY AND AGE

	Status Inconsistency					
Age	Low Ed–High Skill	High Ed–High Skill	Low Ed–Low Skill	High Ed–Low Skill	Total	Tau β
Under 40	19 (152)ª	24 (400)	37 (181)	53 (268)	34 (1,001)	.28**
40 or over	16 (299)	16 (202)	34 (229)	46 (69)	24 (799)	.25*

ª The numbers in parentheses represent the base on which percentages were calculated.
* Significant at the .05 level.
** Significant at the .01 level.

they begin to rationalize, to reduce the pain of the discrepancy between their expectations and their achievements, to find reasons in the constraints or satisfactions of family life for their lack of mobility, to diminish the importance of work in favor of other, more pleasant parts of life; in short, to lower their aspirations and neutralize their dissatisfactions. Table VII-5 shows that dissatisfaction consistently diminishes with age in every category of education and skill; the results are like those in the study by Vollmer, discussed earlier. But even in the face of these accommodations, dissatisfaction remains quite high, especially among better-educated workers. And the increase in dissatisfaction, as one looks from left to right across the rows, remains striking.

Standards for Unhappiness: Relative Deprivation

Americans expect their lives to fulfill the prescriptions about the higher rewards due educated workers, and they expect their incomes and promotion prospects to be in line with those of other similarly situated workers. Their satisfactions, in fact, depend on these expectations. The question is not simply, "Am I deprived?" but "Am I deprived when compared with other men like me?"

Although the sociologists who have used the term "relative deprivation" to describe this phenomenon rarely articulate it, the term reflects the fact that there are no intrinsic, *a priori* criteria for the differential distribution of wealth that are independent of social conventions and the forces that determine them. Differences in income and, to some extent, in social station are thus determined by supply, demand, and power,[12] and the social norms that are reflected in them.

When men decide whether their jobs (and the incomes linked to those jobs) satisfy them, they have little standard to use beyond some sense of their own inner and material needs and the rewards and stations of similar men.

This argument underlies the "status inconsistency" hypothesis developed thus far, but it is possible to carry it a step further, to see if a man is more likely to expect his higher educational level to bring him a more skilled job if men at that level typically hold more skilled jobs. The plant in which a worker is employed would serve as a useful focus for comparison (a "reference group"), but the data did not provide information on the plant level. We therefore moved to industry as a conceivable focus for the worker in evaluating his job. The resulting hypothesis proposes that consistency between education and skill will determine dissatisfaction most in those industries in which increments of skill are most closely tied to increments of education.

To test this notion, industries were characterized by *their* "status consistency"; that is, according to the degree to which

---

[12] This is not the place to discuss the old argument that links rewards to demand and to "society's needs." Suffice it to say that striking sanitation workers in New York City had to let the city *smell* that its need for these workers required it to raise their rewards. These workers still wound up with wages far short of the income of gossip columnists, for example, people who, by some standards, only produce garbage.

TABLE VII-6

PERCENTAGE OF BLUE-COLLAR WORKERS DISSATISFIED,
BY STATUS INCONSISTENCY AND INDUSTRY STATUS CONSISTENCY

Industry Status Consistency[a]	Status Inconsistency				
	Low Ed– High Skill	High Ed– High Skill	Low Ed– Low Skill	High Ed– Low Skill	Total
Low	21 (262)[b]	22 (387)	35 (208)	48 (188)	29 (1,045)
High	12 (188)	22 (215)	36 (202)	57 (149)	30 (754)

[a] Industry status consistency is defined on the basis of the correlation between education and skill. High-consistency industries are those with a high and significant Tau Beta.

[b] The numbers in parentheses represent the base on which percentages were calculated.

skill level is tied to education. Utilizing the relationship between the education and skill levels of the workers in each industry to characterize the industry, a rank-order correlation (Tau Beta) was obtained for each of the 16 industries represented. These industries with high Tau β values between education and skill were characterized as "high consistency" industries; those in which skill level seemed almost unrelated to education were grouped as showing "low consistency."

Table VII-6 shows that the status consistency of industry makes little difference in the proportion of dissatisfied workers among those who *themselves* enjoy consistency with respect to education and skill: those with low education and low skill, and those with high education and high skill (see the two middle columns). The status consistency of the industry does make a big difference among those workers whose own educational achievements are inconsistently higher or lower than their skill level (see the first and last columns).

These two categories, and the life experience that they represent, exert so much influence that they stretch the differences in per cent dissatisfied (around 30 per cent for the population as a whole), from 12 per cent among the less educated men with high-skilled jobs in industries in which higher education is normally required for, or associated with, skilled jobs, to 57 per cent among men with relatively higher educational achievements who do not have skilled jobs although they work in industries in which education usually brings such rewards. Thus when "you need a good education to get a good job," the difference between "making it" despite that system or failing to "make it" despite that system mounts up to a 45 per cent difference.[13]

The results presented by Table VII-6 can be seen in further comparisons of columns 1 and 4. The status consistency of the industry has *opposite* effects for the "low educated, high skill" and the "high educated, low skill" groups. The already low dissatisfaction among the low-education, high-skill group *declines* even further as consistency of industry increases. But the already high dissatisfaction among those with high education and low skill *increases* as consistency of industry increases. Although they are quite unhappy (48 per cent say their job is too simple) in industries in which many similarly educated men are similarly deprived, dissatisfaction increases to 57 per cent in "highly consistent" industries, where most of their better-educated fellows are at higher skill levels than they, and education presumably "counts" in advancement.

[13] Professor David Caplowitz has pointed out that there is a certain amount of statistical constraint in these results: high-consistency industries are by definition industries in which there are few men with little education who have high skill. Thus such men may be exceptional and may differ significantly from similar men in less consistent industries. Similarly, better-educated men who have not reached high-skill jobs in consistent industries may also be strange: they may be characterological "losers" whose under-achievement is justified. However, he concurs that the consistent patterning of the results makes relative deprivation at least as plausible an explanation, and perhaps more plausible, than personal idiosyncrasy. Note that high-education, low-skill men constitute 25 per cent of the entire group (see Table VII-2) and 15 per cent of those in high-consistency industries. Low-education, high-skill men are 19 per cent of the men in consistent industries.

Opportunities

We hedged our predictions about the low-education, low-skilled group while designing these cross-tabulations, recognizing that while their unhappiness might be diminished in "consistent" industries because the "system" explained their lack of advancement, they might, indeed, be less unhappy with jobs in those inconsistent industries where many men with relatively modest education had highly skilled jobs; although their "relative deprivation" could not then be blamed so easily on the system, the opportunity for advancement to a highly skilled job in the same industry might actually exist. Certainly the importance of opportunity for advancement in determining job satisfactions was demonstrated above.

To assess opportunities even approximately we must know the particular educational and skill distribution of jobs within each industry and the consistency with which skilled jobs were tied to educational level. Table VII-7 gives this information.

We see that more of the low-education, low-skill workers are unhappy in low-skill industries (35 per cent and 50 per cent), where their opportunities are few, and that they are most dissatisfied, even more than better-educated workers similarly situated, in those industries whose employees tend to be better educated and in low-skilled jobs. For in these industries these less educated men must compete with better-educated men for scarce skilled jobs. In these industries, on the other hand, the better-educated workers in unskilled jobs, for their part, need suffer less embarassment: though their opportunities are few, other educated men suffer the same deprivation. Here they register the least dissatisfaction.[14]

---

[14] We also attempted to assess the effect of the region by following a procedure similar to that evolved to determine the effect of the industry.

TABLE VII-7

PERCENTAGE OF BLUE-COLLAR WORKERS DISSATISFIED, BY STATUS INCONSISTENCY AND INDUSTRY EDUCATION AND SKILL COMPOSITION

Industry Composition		Status Inconsistency					
Education	Skill	Low Ed– High Skill	High Ed– High Skill	Low Ed– Low Skill	High Ed– Low Skill	Total	Tau β
Low	High	19 (84)[a]	24 (95)	28 (58)	44 (25)	25 (262)	.16
High	High	12 (68)	18 (175)	22 (23)	47 (32)	20 (298)	.21
Low	Low	19 (233)	23 (229)	35 (269)	57 (210)	33 (941)	.30*
High	Low	14 (65)	23 (103)	50 (60)	41 (70)	31 (298)	.18

[a] The numbers in parentheses represent the base on which percentages were calculated.
* Significant at the .01 level.

Technological Complexity and Satisfaction

Professor Blauner, in the study mentioned earlier, concluded that dissatisfaction among the workers in that study could be largely attributed to "job conditions" in "different industries [where] . . . only the levels of training (skill) difference were of an equal magnitude";[15] his analysis was based on workers in four of the 16 industries on which data were available.

We found that although there *are* differences in the percentages of dissatisfied workers according to industry, these differences are not associated with any readily observable *patterns* of differences in the technologies of the industries when all 16 of them are considered. Thus we grouped the 16 industries according to several schemes and discovered that in none of them were the results at all related to the continuum of industries grouped according to worker satisfactions. "Capital intensity" data for these industries during the year of the original Roper study, which might be taken as indicative of technology, did not fit; nor did a continuum of "increasing technology," constructed around production techniques (conceived as "mass production," "batch production," or "unit production") help us to replicate or generalize from Professor Blauner's four-industry model, according to which workers are more satisfied in industries in which they have more control over their work.

Dissatisfactions associated with status inconsistency were greater in large than in small plants, a finding that led us to wonder whether work satisfactions were related to "bureaucratization" in industry. We therefore attempted to create a

---

The results, when controlling for regional education and skill distributions, were ambiguous. The only clearly interpretable feature in the data on region was that the proportion of those dissatisfied continues to increase with increasing personal status inconsistency.

[15] Blauner, *op. cit.*, pp. 11–12, *n.* 16. Again, these are the same workers.

measure of "bureaucratization" by combining the size of companies with information on whether or not they were union shops; the idea was that workers who work in larger, more organized plants are more vulnerable to the power and control of organization. The attempt yielded fuzzy results.[16]

Thus although technological and organizational factors were not clear-cut in their effects, the effect of status consistency remained clear and strong.

As expected, increased education creates (and partially reflects) aspirations for jobs requiring greater skill and holding higher position within the industrial hierarchy. The desire for promotion and the expectation of promotion increase markedly as education increases.

Although the desire for jobs requiring increased skill is widespread, and people with these jobs are more satisfied on each of 15 measures of satisfaction, that desire is even stronger among people with more education, and the frustration of their wish for jobs of increasing complexity produces considerable dissatisfaction.

Job attitudes and aspirations are only somewhat tempered by age and increasing length of service. These "experiences" apparently lead to accommodation (and, presumably to the attrition from the work force, and therefore from the sample, of those with greatest dissatisfaction) but are virtually uninfluenced by other personal background characteristics. So great is the dissatisfaction among people with high education

[16] The relationship between job dissatisfaction and status inconsistency was stronger for union members than for non-union members. We reasoned that there might be relatively higher levels of dissatisfaction among non-union members and that union membership itself might be a way of coping with job dissatisfaction. Once they have organized, however, members' dissatisfactions might be lowered. The data do not permit a test, although they are consistent with such involuted reasoning: among all but the high-education, low-skilled men, non-unionists are relatively more often dissatisfied. It should be noted that the alternative hypothesis and prediction would also have been consistent with our biases: that more dissatisfied men join unions and *remain* dissatisfied. Union members would then be more dissatisfied. The results did not bear this out, however.

and low skill that even when they believe that they will be promoted, their dissatisfaction is considerable.

That stress on the importance of education for advancement tends to aggravate the unhappiness of educated, unskilled men is indicated by the finding that men with high education and low skill are even *more* unhappy in industries where a high association between education and skill exists, and men with limited education and high skill are even *less* dissatisfied.

Although the *magnitudes* of the relationship between "status inconsistency" and job dissatisfaction can be increased or decreased by introducing statistical controls for other background characteristics, for aspirations, for organizational and environmental, or even "reference group" variables, the basic *pattern* of the relationship (dissatisfaction decreasing from high-education, low-skill men through low-education, high-skill men) remains strong, with few exceptions.

These findings suggest that the use of educational credentials as employment criteria are at least as risky as Professor Seymour Harris argued twenty years ago. Other researchers may find, as Professor Harris suggested, that the dissatisfactions of "educated" workers who believe that their jobs are far below those for which their education qualifies them are a genuine threat to the safety of a democratic society. Nothing that has appeared in these data is inconsistent with the formulations of Columbia historian Richard Hofstadter regarding "status politics," frustrations, and the disaffected radical right in America. The rhetoric of employers, meanwhile, gains little support from these data.

Conclusions

The reader may regard the foregoing as a thorough exploration of data too tarnished by age to mean anything for the present and future, a point that deserves some attention. It is at least possible that the date of the original survey (1947) enhances its significance.

Nineteen forty-seven was a boom year. The labor market was as "tight" as in any period in our peacetime history, which suggests that demand produced by World War II had created economic expansion and, with it, some expansion in opportunities to transfer to other jobs, even given the return of millions of World War II veterans to the work force. At no time since that period have employment conditions been so favorable to the worker. In the survey, the men were asked whether they thought it "likely that they would be laid off in the next six months." The effect of status inconsistency was much stronger among men who felt that their jobs were insecure than among those who thought lay-off was unlikely.

In the face of deteriorated employment conditions from 1950 to the mid-1960's, in the face of a steady mass of unemployed workers, in the face, that is, of conditions of increased and continuing job insecurity, the dissatisfactions of the "underutilized" men in this sample must have been at least as severe until the present boom as it was when job insecurities increased dissatisfactions two decades ago.

The stress on education as a public and private panacea developed after these data were collected. The prescription "to get a good job, get a good education" has been thoroughly impressed on today's workers; if they have a good education, they now expect, more than did the men who answered Roper's questionnaire twenty years ago, to get a good job. Our whole argument has been based on the higher expectations of more-educated men and the dissatisfactions resulting from unfulfilled, and unfulfillable, aspirations. These aspirations have probably been heightened since 1947, as the attained education of the work force has grown since 1947, and as the pressure to "stay in school" has accelerated; the effects of increased education and rising aspirations in dissatisfactions, therefore, have probably grown and not diminished with the passing of time.

Moreover, while unskilled positions have been increasing at slower rates in the years since 1947, opportunities for advancement to foreman—let alone to positions "above the foreman level"—have diminished also as management has shown a penchant for hiring college men as foremen, converting industrial top sergeants into second lieutenants. If twenty years ago the belief that they would not be promoted tripled the dissatisfactions of the usually satisfied men with little education but highly skilled jobs and aggravated the dissatisfactions of the low-skill workers to the extent that 65 per cent of them were unhappy, and if twenty years ago 40 per cent of those better-educated, less-skilled men who *did* believe that they would be promoted were dissatisfied in spite of their good prospects, the unhappiness must be profound indeed for present-day blue-collar workers, whose education is even higher and who have heard and believed the promises made to diploma-holders.

One final test of management's rhetoric, and by implication of formulations concerning the value of education, may be made by exploring the job experiences of public employees. As a consequence of various public policies, civil servants and military personnel, compared to other employees, are somewhat less likely to hold their jobs because of their educational achievements. In the next chapter, therefore, some of the tables, literally and figuratively, are turned in a discussion of data on thousands of military personnel and on a 5-per-cent sample of nearly 200,000 civil servants.

VIII Education and Public Service

The growing concern of Americans with home rule, decentralization, and participatory democratic forms reminds us of the significance of public bureaucracies in the social, political, and economic life of the nation. The tragedy of Vietnam, the degeneration of the measures against poverty, the battles of city dwellers against negligent educators, the struggle of some law-enforcement champions against the enforcement of civil rights, the passionate crusades of students against government contracts with multiversities, all have triggered explosions on the Left and Right against the policies, practices, and strategies of government at all levels. Presidents, mayors, social workers, teachers, chancellors, generals, cabinet secretaries, police officers, human-rights commissioners, and professors have been loudly condemned by offended citizens of this nation, which maintains its historic links to populism and the pastoral romanticism that has informed its curious politics.

Although the criticisms and accusations pertaining to government may deserve more careful and dispassionate scrutiny than they are likely to receive when the times are out of joint, the *fact* of the growth of the so-called public sector can hardly be denied. And whatever the other consequences may be, the implications for manpower analysis of burgeoning public work forces cannot be ignored.

Consider that as long ago as 1963, or 18 months before the war in Vietnam was substantially escalated and a full year before the public virtually voted *down* the war in a presidential election, 16 of every 100 employed Americans worked for one of their various governments. We can speculate about what would have happened to this statistic had not the victorious candidates opposed an expansion of the war effort.

The attacks on the educational and defense establishments, in the meantime, have closely paralleled the very substantial manpower expansion in these two areas of public activity:

> During the decade of the 1930's, employment by the federal government (including persons on work relief as well as those in the Armed Forces) was the chief source of expansion. From 1950 to 1963, however, it was the increasing employment offered by state and local governments which accounted for the major share of the expansion in government employment. . . .
>
> When we review government employment by function, without regard to the level of government, we learn that employment for national defense purposes has been the single most important activity since 1940 . . . . Education was in second place in each benchmark year, and since 1954 it has become increasingly important as a field of government employment.[1]

Although attacks on government have illuminated the political problems that preoccupy the Left and Right, they have obscured manpower and employment developments that heartened more conventional liberals and conservatives for a time. In this connection, we recall that, in the last months of President Kennedy's tenure and the early years of President Johnson's administration, a politically moderate consensus was organized around the so-called new economics; according to one part of this Keynesian logic, the public services were regarded as an apposite arena in the effort to expand employment opportunities, particularly for disadvantaged Americans. While some sought to have government become "the em-

---

[1] Eli Ginzberg, Dale L. Hiestand, and Beatrice G. Reubens, *The Pluralistic Economy* (New York: McGraw-Hill, 1965), p. 120.

ployer of last resort," others pursued what their critics casti-
gated as a program of vulgar pragmatism.

Daniel P. Moynihan, a former Assistant Secretary of Labor,
and currently a member of President Nixon's cabinet, argued
for a time that the Armed Forces should be utilized as an ad-
junct to manpower programs. Youngsters from low-income
families, he contended, could get a start on work careers by
participating in the military and would simultaneously acquire
the discipline and skills required of young servicemen on active duty. This argument had the support of the former Secretary of Defense Robert McNamara. The war "shouldn't be
a total loss." It was argued further, that civilian positions in
the government could more readily be staffed by disadvantaged Americans because federal and state civil services pre-
clude discriminatory employment practices.

An examination of the correlates of education among public
employees is significant in a society in which public employment is regularly utilized as an instrument to distribute or re-
distribute work opportunities. The fact that he deplores the
existence of large military forces and the destructive work in
which they are engaged need not deter the analyst from using
available data to cast light on the subject of the present study.

As it turns out, sufficient data are available on military
personnel, on a 5-per-cent sample of the entire federal civil
service, and on the highly skilled employees of one major
federal agency to expand the discussion of issues explored in
previous chapters. The performance and educational achievements of military personnel are a convenient starting point.

The Armed Forces

America's defense establishment, left to its own resources,
would probably elevate educational achievement to the same

place in the scheme of manpower policy accorded it by civilian employers. Indeed, the difficulties of manpower specialists at the upper reaches of this considerable pyramid of skills and numbers are compounded by deferment policies and the attitudes of most better-educated Americans, as well as by the personnel policies of civilian employers. Army manpower specialists would prefer to be spared the task of training "what's left" to them by American society, which has managed in recent decades to fight its wars, hot as well as cold, with a relatively small proportion of the nation's labor force; they would prefer to recruit and select people in accordance with their professional judgment.

It is precisely the fact that the military does *not* enjoy the specific labor-market advantages of private employers that makes the military experience relevant to the present study.[2] In addition to front-line combatants, modern warfare requires an enormous number of specialists whose skills represent a microcosm of the larger civilian system of employment. In the circumstances of the Defense Department, the military branches are obligated to train individuals to fit a vast, changing, and complex series of occupations, many of which have civilian equivalents.

Stories of military inefficiency are legion, of course, and have inspired countless songs, plays, novels, and films, both serious and comic. But the war machine does run, and it does so because men (and women) learn to navigate, type, and fly, to cook, grease motors, repair trucks, airplanes, and electronic equipment, to sort men, materiel, and mail, and to perform myriad other tasks. The military may justifiably take credit for doing its work as well as it does considering the magnitude of its task and, its spokesmen would add, the limited choice it has in selecting its personnel!

---

[2] The military does enjoy the comparative advantage of being guaranteed the *availability* of the "force levels" approved by Congress; these levels are always lower, however, than military manpower planners wish.

Fortunately for present purposes, all the military services have embarked on systematic efforts to develop and validate their techniques for assigning military personnel to military occupations. Personnel laboratories in each branch have designed a multitude of "screening" tests, the results of which can be combined with data about the backgrounds of a large segment of young American males for an analysis of individual performance.[3] In these ventures, knowledge of the educational achievements of military personnel typically adds little—sometimes nothing—to an effort to predict success in any of the Armed Services.

The performance measures used in many of these studies are inevitably inadequate in one way or another. Only a few studies bear upon general military "suitability"—that is, soldiers', sailors', and airmen's adaptation to the military life and their ability to survive without organizationally disruptive behavior.[4] Similarly, only a few studies have been conducted in which actual performance in the field, in combat, or on the job has been measured. Such undertakings require research designs permitting analysts to deal with standardized evaluations by trained raters working in controlled, homogeneous settings, and these conditions obviously are not easily met.

The results that *can* be reported are interesting, however, for they are based on performance records that may well relate to actual behavior in military billets. Most of these measures are based on the scores and grades that various personnel have achieved in training programs that take job tasks as well as pencil-and-paper examination grades into account. Electronic technicians, for example, are graded on their trouble-

[3] We are indebted to Dr. Harold Wool, until recently Assistant Secretary of Defense, who gave generously of his time and advice in the early stages of the research. He is, of course, in no way responsible for the use made here of data procured through his good offices, nor has he had any opportunity to review drafts of the present discussion.

[4] The normative question here of whether such adaptation is good or bad is begged. From a military viewpoint, of course, maladaptive behavior is undesirable.

shooting and repair skills as well as on written tests. These measures are in the same universe of measures as those used by private employers who generally see school success as a prerequisite to job performance.

In most of the relevant military studies, investigators have been concerned with improving the validity of classification and aptitude tests, or of items used in the construction of these tests, in conjunction with background information, in screening personnel for assignment to the hundreds of courses, long and short, that train them for military occupational specialties. While cynics may scoff at the utility of such tests—and few are the veterans who do not recall the "catch 22's" that made PX entrepreneurs out of experienced civilian sanitation workers—the researchers in military personnel laboratories have gone far in their efforts indeed.

In one of the first relevant post-World War II studies of Air Force personnel, high-school graduates, who at the time made up from 14 to 50 per cent of the monthly "input" of airmen, were compared with nongraduates in their performance on the Army Classification Tests and on 13 tests which were subsequently to make up the earliest Airman Classification Battery.[5] Dr. Dailey concluded that "high-school graduation, unless supplemented by other screening measures such as tests or the careful review of the actual high school record, does not insure that a basic trainee will be of high potential usefulness to the Air Force."[6]

Another investigator had noted that high-school graduates were not uniformly or markedly superior to nongraduates: the score distributions for the two groups overlapped on every test.[7] Nevertheless, the formal educational achievements of

[5] J. T. Dailey, "Comparison of High School Graduates and Nongraduates Among Recruits in the Indoctrination Division of the Air Training Command," Psychological Research and Examining Unit, Air Training Command, *Research Bulletin 48–2*, March, 1948.

[6] *Ibid.*, p. 18.

[7] See William B. Lecznar, "Years of Education as a Predictor of Technical Training Success," Technical Documentary Report PRL-TDR 64-2, 6570th

airmen do appear to be related to their military suitability. According to a 1956 study by a senior Air Force investigator, high-school graduates have a lower probability of being discharged as unsuitable than high-school "dropouts,"[8] a finding that reflects the fact that "dropout" populations usually contain disproportionately more young people with low I.Q.'s and other "deficiencies."[9] In an extension of this study, investigators at Lackland Air Force Base were able to develop an equation, using data on age, years of education, and an aptitude index, for predicting the probabilities of discharge for unsuitability of the airmen included in the 1956 study.[10]

The findings in another study, however, indicate that the results of the 1956 study might have been influenced by the way in which education was treated methodologically. When education is treated as a dichotomous variable—that is, when discrete levels of educational achievements are considered simply, such as "high-school graduate" vs. "non–high-school graduate"—it may do some violence to education in the equations derived by the statistical technique known as regression analysis.

In 1963 Leland Brockaw undertook an extensive study of 4,458 graduates of eight technical military courses in order

---

Personnel Research Laboratory, Aerospace Medical Division, AF Systems Command (Lackland AFB, Texas, 1964).

[8] E. S. Flyer, "Factors Relating to Discharge for Unsuitability Among 1956 Airman Accessions to the Air Force," WADC-TN-59-201, DDC Document AD-230 758 (Lackland AFB, Texas: Personnel Laboratory, Wright Air Development Center, December, 1959).

[9] S. M. Miller *et al.*, *School Dropouts: A Commentary and Annotated Bibliography* (Syracuse: Syracuse University Youth Development Center, 1964), pp. 31–77. It should be noted that in this particular work, however, there is considerable variation from one community to another in the capabilities of dropouts. In 1945-46, 5 per cent of youths who left school in the Midwest had I.Q.'s above 114; in another example, 30 per cent of St. Paul, Minn., dropouts had I.Q.'s above 100.

[10] W. E. Fisher *et al.*, "Prediction of Unsuitability Discharges," WADD-TN-60-260, DDC Document AD-24807 (Lackland AFB, Texas: Personnel Laboratory, Wright Air Development Division, October, 1960); and Lecznar, *op. cit.*, p. 3.

... to evaluate a system of classification for assignment to technical school using aptitude information and reasonably comprehensive information on educational level, experience, and achievement . . . [and] to determine whether a brief questionnaire devoted solely to educational topics would be of sufficient validity to permit its use, in addition to the Airman Qualifying Examination, . . . in appraising a prospective enlistee as a desirable addition to the Air Force . . . .[11]

Brockaw's data are based on 16 questions about the characteristics of the courses and schools that the graduates of eight service programs had attended prior to military service and about their educational achievements. His techniques permitted him to establish the statistical weights of these items because they allocated the variability in final military technical-school grades achieved by the graduates among each of the separate and combined items used in the equation.

Brockaw's findings on the effect of educational achievement appear in Table VIII-1. The data reveal that there is a modest but positive relationship between high-school completion and course grades in only three of the eight programs. Several of these courses, it should be noted, are for occupations for which there are obvious civilian equivalents.

In addition, Brockaw computed two sets of mulitple correlations—between course grades for each technical program and "High School Graduation," and between grades and a

[11] Leland D. Brockaw, "Prediction of Success in Technical Training from Self-Report Information on Educational Achievement," AF System Command TD Report PRL-TDR-63-11 (Lackland AFB, Texas: Personnel Research Laboratory, Aerospace Medical Division, April, 1963), p. 1. The Airman Qualifying Examination is a screening device used by Air Force recruiters. The findings reported do not prove a great deal about tests. In many ways such tests can be almost as discriminatory as formal educational requirements, since many of them "measure" precisely what educational experiences are calculated to evoke: achievements of an intellectual nature. One must consider the data in this chapter, then, in light of qualifications that this footnote implies: the studies are interesting in that they apply to a selected and restricted population upon whom the tests are standardized and for whom, therefore, they are "valid."

Table VIII-1

CORRELATION OF EDUCATIONAL ACHIEVEMENT WITH FINAL SCHOOL GRADE IN EIGHT AIR FORCE TECHNICAL TRAINING COURSES

Educational Achievement[a]	Technical School Course[b]							
	A	B	C	D	E	F	G	H
Grade school or less	—04	—10	—09	00	—04	06	—06	—05
Some high school	—30	—22	—28	—19	—22	—14	—31	—25
High-school graduate	23	24	26	01	00	01	15	12
Some college	18	12	08	14	21	12	17	18
College graduate	09	00	12	03	10	05	06	11
Number	738	690	593	267	820	554	759	433

[a] Each educational category is treated as a dichotomized variable; those with the education specified by the category are against all others.

[b] The courses, identified by letters in the column headings, are as follows: A-Reciprocating Engine Mechanic, B-Munitions Specialist, C-Organizational Supply Specialist, D-Accounting and Finance Specialist, E-Weather Observer, F-Control Tower Operator, G-Aircraft Radio Repairman, H-Fire Control System Mechanic.

SOURCE: Excerpted from Brockaw, op. cit., Appendixes I and II, pp. 7–8.

"Selector Aptitude Index." The Aptitude Index showed uniformly higher predictive values than the education variable. When the two were combined, however, they produced "highly significant improvements in predictive efficiency." Brockaw concludes that information about educational achievement makes a significant contribution to an effort to predict technical-school success.[12]

The data in the tables lead us to interpret the word "significant" only in the narrowest statistical sense, however. Had it been possible to employ educational achievement as a five-step ladder corresponding to the items in Table VIII-1, rather than as five separate, dichotomized variables, the curvilinear character of the relationships suggested in Table VIII-1 would probably have modified the later correlation results quiet a bit. By splitting educational achievements into five *pairs* (e. g., high-school graduation *versus* all other categories, item 3)

[12] Brockaw, op. cit., Table 2, p. 4.

and treating the pairs separately, a great many of the realities of the results are lost. That the researcher did not notice this methodological problem is suggested by his unqualified observation that educational achievements add to his effort to make predictions; the facts are not so clear.

Even if we concede that increments of educational achievement contribute to the prospect that a young man will be found suitable for military service, the data in Brockaw's study suggest that these increments contribute relatively little to his prospects in technical programs. This, indeed, is the consistent finding in studies of the graduates of no fewer than 95 other technical schools and programs; in one such study, of 34 schools, the students involved numbered 11,408. In all of these studies, aptitude tests not unlike those employed in Brockaw's study correlate well with proficiency and performance scores, while educational achievements rarely account for more than 4 per cent of the variations in these measures of students' capabilities.[13]

In an unpublished memorandum, L. G. Humphrey, another Air Force researcher, commented on some of these numerous studies as follows:

> Years of education are:
> a) only moderately related to objective measures of aptitude;
> b) a poor predictor of success in training;
> c) almost unrelated to objective measures of proficiency on the job. . . .
> Within the Air Force, completion of high school is thus not a useful criterion for assignment to school or on the job. . . .
> It is believed that the relative insignificance of years of education for Air Force classification and assignment purposes is due to a changing philosophy of education which:
> a) promotes children in accordance with chronological age rather than achievement;

[13] See Lecznar, *op. cit.*, p. 2, *n.* 2 and 3, p. 9, and pp. 11–14; and L. D. Brockaw, "Suggested Composition of Airman Classification Instruments," WADD-TN-60-214, DDC Document AD-252 252 (Lackland AFB, Texas: Personnel Laboratory, Wright Air Development Division, August, 1960).

b) provides a curriculum varied by type and difficulty level to fit the abilities of all the children in the school.

The apparent trend is toward less predictability from years of education rather than more.[14]

This last observation is particularly interesting because it is based on data that bear directly on the assumptions informing conventional judgments about education.

Of course, Air Force data do not tell us that education is unimportant or that formal learning experiences are irrelevant to the capacities, intellectual or otherwise, of the hundreds of thousands of men whose personnel histories are regularly reviewed at Lackland Air Force Base. Rather, these data point to the folly of confusing a man's driver's license with his driving ability. Just as different communities have different safety standards and variable skill requirements, so schools and school systems vary in their policies and practices. It should surprise no one that credentials alone predict performance so poorly. In none of the Air Force's studies does educational achievement account for more than a marginal portion of the substantial variations observed in the performance of very sizable numbers of airmen who have completed a large number of the most diversified courses.

The Navy's experience is entirely in line with that of the Air Force, although there are some variations in Navy personnel studies that make them immediately relevant. The Armed Forces have, for example, experimented with "salvage" programs in which illiterates and men who earn low scores on military classification tests are given remedial training to compensate for shortcomings attributable to social and other factors. These efforts have been uniformly successful; graduates develop into useful servicemen as often as the "average" and "normal" members of control groups with which they have been regularly compared.[15] Indeed, remarkably favorable

---

[14] Cited in Lecznar, *op. cit.*, p. 3.

[15] See Eli Ginzberg and Douglas Bray, *The Uneducated* (New York: Columbia University Press, 1953); S. Goldberg, "Psychological Procedures

changes in the adaptation and performance of low test-scorers have been produced through "recruit preparatory training" (RPT). In some instances these low-scoring candidates with modest educational backgrounds have performed at higher levels than better-educated men with higher GCT scores.[16] And, in a 1955 study, educational achievements were found not to be related to the performance of 1,370 Navy recruits who attended an RPT course. Neither were they related to the grades recruits received from their company commanders and instructors, nor to successes and failures in completing recruit training.[17]

On a related matter, the results are equally intriguing. A study of re-enlistment rates—always a vital figure to the military and to the Selective Service apparatus—revealed that re-enlistment rates of "acceptable" naval personnel were nearly twice as high for those who had completed less than twelve years of school as for those who had completed twelve or more years.[18] This finding, paralleling the earlier one that the job experience of better-educated workers in many private firms is

---

Employed in the Army's Special Training Units," *Journal of Clinical Psychology*, I (1945), 118–25; E. P. Hagen and R. L. Thorndike, "A Study of the World War II Navy Careers of Naval Personnel," Washington, D.C., *Research Report* Contract Hour-644, April, 1953; S. Mastropaolo *et al.*, "A Study of the Relative Effects of Six-Week and Twelve-Week Experimental Training Programs on a Sample of Limited Aptitude Airmen," Technical Report 54-36 (Lackland AFB, Texas: AF Personnel and Training Research Center, September, 1954).

[16] See C. N. Cofer, *Adjustment to Recruit Training: A Study of the Effects of Recruit Preparatory Training*. Technical Bulletin 54-22 (Washington: Bureau of Naval Personnel, December, 1954). This is a revealing study of considerable relevance to discussions of the "youth problem" in the "war against poverty." It also contains an answer, by implication, to civilian employers who claim that high-school dropouts have uncorrectable defects in their personal attitudes and capacity for disciplined work.

[17] See Janet Eells, *Evaluation of Screening Standards for Recruit Preparatory Training*, Technical Bulletin 55-11 (San Diego, Calif.: U.S. Naval Personnel Research Field Activity, June, 1955).

[18] Personnel Measurement Division, "Factors Affecting Re-enlistment of First Enlistees," Naval Personnel 18497; W2006.2.7 (Washington: U.S. Naval Personnel Research Field Activity, May, 1966).

shorter than that of their less educated coworkers, is probably related to the fact that the civilian economy does not favor ex-servicemen with modest educational achievements; many of these men re-enlist to exploit their military gains and to avoid labor-market disabilities.

Other Navy studies are virtual replications of those conducted by the Air Force. A study correlating the educational achievements of 415 electronic technicians with their proficiency scores on each of 17 concrete tasks, in conjunction with their age and pay grades (which is to say, the experience of these skilled men), found that educational achievements were *negatively* (though not significantly) associated with performance. The reseacher suggests that the negative signs of the correlations, reported in Table VIII-2, are

. . . probably a reflection of [the] changing patterns of education in the United States. On the average, men entering the Navy in recent years have completed more time in school than men who entered the Navy several years ago. Since men with several years of experience, on the average, have higher check-list scores than their younger associates, the relationships between years of education completed and derived scores tend to be negative.[19]

These data take on added significance from the facts that (1) there is a high correlation between proficiency on the 17 tasks as measured by the technicians' *own* estimates and the ratings these technicians received from their supervisors on ships and posts in the two "theaters"; and (2) there is a tendency for re-enlistments to be higher among those who entered the Navy at a relatively young age than for those who were better educated and therefore entered the Navy when they were older.

[19] Adolph V. Anderson, *Training, Utilization and Proficiency of Navy Electronics Technicians II*. Technical Bulletin 62-13, *Technical Experience and Proficiency* (San Diego, Calif.: U.S. Naval Personnel Research Field Activity, September, 1962).

TABLE VIII-2

CORRELATIONS BETWEEN DERIVED CHECK-LIST SCORES
AND AGE, EDUCATION, AND PAY GRADE

Check-List Score	Age		Education		Pay Grade	
	PACFLT[a]	CONUS[b]	PACFLT	CONUS	PACFLT	CONUS
Basic measurements	26	24	−06	−05	38	26
Basic troubleshooting	33	43	−12	−15	52	58
Computation	32	29	−07	−17	47	39
Replace basic components	34	40	−08	−23	48	47
Records maintenance	42	65	−04	−08	50	68
Radio & teletype POMSEE[e]	20	24	−04	−08	29	22
Communications measurements	37	32	−11	−14	49	41
Communications check	33	29	−08	−11	44	38
Communications troubleshooting	36	20	−08	−12	45	36
Radar & Loran POMSEE	26	33	−10	−19	34	41
Radar measurements	26	33	−10	−23	38	53
Radar check, adjust, align	32	33	−13	−20	43	50
Radar troubleshooting	37	36	−12	−23	48	52
Use of an oscilloscope	41	41	−12	−21	51	55
Use of a VOM[d]	25	20	−03	−16	39	29
Use of a VTVM[e]	33	32	−05	−18	42	40
Use of a signal generator	32	30	−12	−10	46	45

[a] Pacific Fleet-based sailors.
[b] Continental United States-based sailors.
[c] Performance, Operation, and Maintenance Standards for Electronic Equipment.
[d] Volt Ohm Ammeter.
[e] Vacuum Tube Voltmeter.
SOURCE: Anderson, *op. cit.*, Table II, p. 18.

In a later report on the same investigation, the researchers examined the results of field tests of the competence of these electronic technicians asked to repair four different types of complex electronic testing equipment. The outcome was the same as reported in the study of the 17 tasks performed in the electronics training-school program:[20] experience is much more significant than formal education in accounting for performance in this demanding skill area.

Finally, David Kipnis reports that a "hand skills test" is a valuable supplementary screening device among lower-aptitude servicemen. An observed willingness to persist in tiring tasks, beyond minimum standards, contributed to both the school performance and the job performance (as measured by supervisors' evaluations) of low-aptitude men, but not of high-aptitude men, whose performance was better predicted by aptitude-test scores. The results of a study of 135 enlisted radiomen, 240 nuclear-power men, and 108 officer candidates indicate that less educated low-aptitude men may perform as well as high-aptitude personnel. These less educated men compensate for what would otherwise be deficiencies in their capacities for sustained effort.[21]

This review of Air Force and Navy data has perhaps been sufficiently detailed to spare the reader exposure to similar Army studies. This branch, too, has sought to rationalize further the selection of candidates for assignment to school and, in common with other branches, has produced many revealing statistics. In a 1967 communication to the writer, Dr. J. E. Uhlaner, Director of Laboratories, U. S. Army Personnel Research Office, Department of the Army, notes that the Army's Personnel Laboratory has for years sought to make the Army Classification Battery a more valid device for personnel assignment. Toward this end, the Laboratory compared

20 *Ibid.*, Part III.
21 David Kipnis, *Prediction of Performance Among Lower Aptitude Men*, Technical Bulletin 61-10 (Washington: U.S. Naval Personnel Field Research Activity, July, 1961).

enlisted men's test scores on this battery with their formal educational achievements in conjunction with performance in Army schools of all kinds. The "formal education" variable, he writes,

> . . . may be dismissed . . . . [Its] validity coefficients . . . were substantially less than the magnitude of the coefficients for the more valid ACB [Army Classification Battery] tests.
>
> After obtaining the above findings for occupational group after group in our prediction studies, we stopped mentioning the variable of years of education in our reports, although it is still included in the design.

In addition to the "salvage" programs and the validation studies already reported, data are available from another type of experiment applicable to all the Armed Forces. These findings confirm the judgment that when conventional screening standards are lowered, even substantially, no dire implications for performance ensue.

In the fall of 1966, the Department of Defense began accepting men who would not have met earlier mental or educational standards (95 per cent) or who had easily correctable physical defects (5 per cent). These men are trained in familiar fashion.

> While entrance standards have been revised, performance standards have not been lowered. The New Standards men are being trained right alongside other men in our regular training centers and schools. They are not singled out or stigmatized in any manner. Any special assistance they may require is provided as part of the normal training process. After completion of basic training, they are trained in a military skill either through formal courses or by on-the-job training.[22]

[22] Project 100,000: Characteristics and Performance of "New Standards" Men (Washington: Office of the Assistant Secretary of Defense, Manpower and Reserve Affairs, July, 1968), p. iv. The population this progress report considers actually numbers 125,152.

While the failure rates of New Standards men in advanced skill-training programs are higher than those of the control group with which they were compared, these rates have been dropping as a result of improvements in assignment procedures and training courses. And where 98 per cent of the control group successfully completed basic training, the corresponding figure for New Standards men is 96 per cent. About half of the small group that fails are discharged for medical reasons, primarily for conditions that existed prior to induction. Sixty-two per cent of these men are assigned to noncombat skill groups, most of which have direct or related counterparts in the civilian economy—food service, supply, wire communications, motor transport, and automotive repair.

That all groups of New Standards men do well in the service may be inferred from their progression up the military rank structure. Compared with other men, they are, according to the Assistant Secretary of Defense, "making very satisfactory progress." Eighty-four per cent reached the third pay rank, and nearly half reached the fourth, within the first 16.5 months of active service. The figures for the control group were 93 per cent and 64 per cent, respectively. "The gap in pay grade between New Standards men and control-group men is greatest in the Navy," according to the report, and "in part, this is due to the fact that in the Navy most New Standards men receive skill training 'on-the-job' instead of attending a formal school and thereby take longer to qualify for promotion."[23]

The military experience, which has been far more thoroughly documented than that of the so-called private sector, is substantially subversive of the prevailing ideologies that make so much of marginal increments of formal education. The results are interesting, not only because they include data bearing on relatively skilled occupational specialties, but

[23] *Ibid.*, p. vii.

because they are suggestive of the productive potential of a labor market in a nation in which there has been chronic unemployment and, apparently, underemployment of large numbers of men and women with allegedly deficient educational credentials.

Consider, too, that the experience of the military* is not altogether unlike that of the civilian economy during wartime. When the labor market is "tight," as it almost always is for the Department of Defense with respect to all but minority-group members of the labor force, people are hired less selectively, and with results that are largely gratifying. It can hardly be an inspiration to the unemployed youths of the 1960's and '70's to know that they have few deficiencies when their country needs soldiers but that they are otherwise expendable human beings. Were they to accept such a judgment with equanimity they would surely be faulted for their lack of initiative and for their stupidity.

That "dipping lower into the manpower barrel"—an unfortunate phrase used even by intelligent informants during the course of this investigation—is costly to productivity and efficiency is an argument with a slightly hollow ring in view of the data on the military's apparent ability to do well "with what it gets."

When we turn to civilian public servants, the data, like those on employees in the private sector, tend to be fuzzier. Civilians, whether in public or private employment, are rarely trained and indoctrinated in *formal* ways for *specified* technical tasks; consequently there are no data precisely paralleling those on performance in military-school programs. The data in the next section on the careers of a number of different government employees are nevertheless revealing, for they cut into the problem of educational credentials in yet another way. The fact that they contain detailed information on civil servants' promotions makes these data especially valuable.

Civilian Employees

Managers in government, no less than other managers, are eager to recruit qualified personnel for agencies with an internal labor market from which people can be selected to move up to more responsible positions; few organizations benefit from personnel programs in which all openings are filled from the "outside." To this end, voices are often heard proclaiming the need to obtain better—i.e., more educated—civil servants.

In New York City in 1966, for example, the Mayor's Task Force on City Personnel, after emphasizing the need "to identify, develop, and advance outstanding executive talent within its own ranks," found that "recent college graduates are now effectively excluded from management positions because these positions are filled almost entirely by promotion from clerical grades." The Task Force thereupon recommended that "the Mayor . . . stimulate the use of college graduates and persons with advanced degrees."[24] Such recruitment efforts in the public service are often complicated by the constraints imposed by a variety of policies designed to reduce, if not eliminate, formal requirements that operate effectively to discriminate unlawfully against one or another group of citizens. At the same time there may be policies of perferential treatment—as toward discharged servicemen—that confound efforts to use conventional hiring standards, including educational criteria, for many jobs. Finally, the use of competitive examinations may leave substantially open the question of the manner in which a job applicant *prepares* for government work.

[24] "Highlights from the Mayor's Task Force Reports," *City Almanac: A Bulletin of the Metropolitan Information Service* (New York: New School for Social Research, Center for New York City Affairs, 1966) I, 4, Section 2, unpaginated.

All this is to say that while educational credentials may be explicitly required for some jobs (for example, medical degrees for public-health positions) and implicitly required for other jobs (presumably only a law-school graduate will be able to pass a state bar examination and qualify for a variety of legal jobs in government), it is not necessary to attend college or high school to pass general informational tests, for which disciplined reading and native intelligence may be more than adequate. The upshot is that many federal and state civil-service positions are held by people who have not completed their studies for the standard diplomas and degrees awarded graduates of high schools and colleges.

In the face of this fact, it is useful to examine the determinants of promotion in government to see whether the career experiences of educated employees reflect their investments in their training; at the same time, their career experiences should also reflect their performance if a merit system is operative. The cooperation of the U.S. Civil Service Commission, which made it possible to construct a randomly selected 5 per cent sample of 180,000 males that is largely representative of the males among the 2.5 million federal employees, has facilitated such an examination.[25]

Promotion rates were defined by calculating the number of civil-service grades elapsed between entry grades and grades at the time of the study, and dividing the resulting number by the subjects' length of service in government.[26] The conse-

---

[25] The data were orginally collected in a larger Civil Service study; the data on male personnel from GS-5 through GS-15 jobs were retained for present purposes. We acknowledge our debt to the Civil Service Commissioner, Mr. John W. Macy, and to Drs. Albert P. Maslow and David L. Futransky for providing the data and their help and advice. They are, of course, in no way responsible for the ways in which the materials were processed or analyzed.

[26] It was necessary to analyze separately those who entered service at GS grades 1–4, 5–10, and 1–14. Since only GS-5 employees and above were sampled in the original survey, those who began at GS 1–4 had obviously received promotions to get into the sample, but for those in GS 5 and above, it was possible to have received no promotions. The GS-11–14 group suffer

TABLE VIII-3

ANNUAL PROMOTION RATES AND VARIATION EXPLAINED
BY PREDICTORS,[a] MALES IN THE FEDERAL CIVIL SERVICE,
BY ENTRY GRADE (1963)

| | Entry Civil Service Grade | | |
	GS 1–4	GS 5–10	GS 11–14
Annual promotion rate			
Mean	.23	.26	.15
Standard deviation	.11	.16	.16
Per cent of variation in promotion rate explained by:			
Length of service	23.1%	4.3%	3.2%
Age	—	10.0	4.4
Current occupation	10.8	7.6	5.6
Education	3.2	3.3	6.8
In-service training	2.2	1.0	1.5
Number of agencies	—	—	1.1
Duty location	—	—	.8
Total variation explained	39.3%	26.2%	23.4%
Number	(4,204)	(3,182)	(481)

[a] Automatic Interaction Detector Program.

quent rates were then divided into the portions that arise from each of ten sources that were considered *a priori* to have a bearing on promotion. These "sources" included educational achievement, seniority, type of occupation (accounting, administration, clerical work, etc.), and other items, including organizational as well as personal characteristics.

The results, corroborating those of private firms reported earlier, appear in Table VIII-3.[27] Except for the group in GS

a ceiling effect; those promoted beyond GS 15 would not appear in the sample. Since it is rare for people to enter at GS 11 or higher, this is an idiosyncratic, more educated group.

[27] The computer work and the detailed analysis from which these results stem were accomplished by Gretchen Maclachlan, of Columbia University's Conservation of Human Resources Project. This effort, which was an extraordinarily exacting one, required a number of inventive trials and readjustments. It is a pleasure to acknowledge her technical expertise, her patience, and her helpful judgments on innumerable methodological issues.

grades 11–14, length of service and age are far more significant than education in accounting for the promotion rates of civil servants. For the GS-1–4 group, the ten factors together accounted for over 39 per cent of the variance in promotion rates, while length of service, by itself, accounted for fully 23 per cent. When age and length of service are considered together, as a surrogate measure of experience, the combination becomes the strongest factor in accounting for the promotion rates of the highest level, the GS 11–14 category, as well.

Generally speaking, promotions come early in the careers of civil servants, partly as a function of the shape of the hierarchy of GS ranks in government organizations. After long service (or, as in the case of GS 5–10's, age), the early advantages of educational achievement are cancelled out. Men of 39 years of age or over have about the same promotion rates regardless of education. This finding is remarkable when we consider that formal educational achievements are quite relevant to the work of some civil servants. A law degree, for example, is relevant to the work of National Labor Relations Board examiners; undergraduate training in the natural sciences is a reasonable background for a variety of jobs in the laboratories of the National Institutes of Health. Such "realistic" educational preparations should inject some upward bias in the role of education in promotion rates; the effect of educational achievement is nevertheless attenuated over a relatively short time.

Occupation is the second most significant factor in determining the promotion rates of the two lowest GS groups, accounting for 11 and 8 per cent, respectively. Among the highest-level personnel, the statistical influence of occupation is exceeded in importance only by that of educational achievement. Since educational credentials are more likely to have

The computer program used was the Automatic Interaction Detector (AID); see J. A. Sonquist and J. N. Morgan, *The Detection of Interaction Effects* (SRC Monograph 35, Institute for Social Research, University of Michigan, 1964).

been a factor in the hiring of the GS 11–14's than of the two other groups, however, this result is hardly surprising.

That educational achievement does survive this quantitative screening process in a fashion at all consistent with the conventional wisdom regarding education cannot be denied. It accounts, however, for a very small portion—3 per cent in the two lowest groups—of the observed rates of promotion for the employees in this large sample. In all, experience and occupation far outweigh educational achievement in determining the promotion rates of this large sample of civil servants.

Since educational achievements are highly correlated with the grades at which these government workers entered public service,[28] and since entry grade is closely related to the current grade of the subjects (Tau Beta $= .22$), the slightly more rapid advancements of the relatively better-educated men are a function of the boost that comes from being *hired* into higher ranks upon entering government services.

Thus, in Table VIII-4, it is clear from the first column that the over-all relationship between education and current grade, from which the force of education might be inferred, is reduced substantially when the civil-service entry grades of the subjects are held constant. Since the relationship between educational achievement and entry grade is stronger than that between education and current grade, controlled for entry grade,[29] the inference may be drawn that education has a greater bearing on the entry grades of these public servants than on their eventual promotion prospects. And, since education and entry grade are positively related while the relationship between education and current grade decreases for each successively higher entry grade, it is apparent that promotion experience is a function of these workers' *starting* points in the GS hierarchy.

---

[28] Tau $\beta = .32$, significant at the .01 level.
[29] The GS 1-4's are the exception (see p. 162, *n*. 26, in which this problem was anticipated).

TABLE VIII-4

THE EFFECTS OF EDUCATION AND LENGTH OF SERVICE
ON CURRENT GRADE, MALES IN THE FEDERAL CIVIL SERVICE,
BY ENTRY GRADE

| | Tau β Between | | |
Entry Grade	Education and Current GS	Length of Service and Current GS	Number
1–4	.31**	.31**	4,553
5–6	.32**	.47**	1,860
7–8	.26**	.51**	1,215
9–10	.24**	.45**	580
11	.22*	.50**	265
12	.02	.37**	153
13	.18	.40	77
14	.26	.10	21
All entry grades	.34**	.22**	8,724

* Significant at the .05 level.
** Significant at the .01 level.

To put this in another way, the better-educated civil servant is more likely to be hired at a relatively high grade, and the higher his grade at entry, the less relevant education will be to his prospects for promotion. In Table VIII-4, the statistical effects of educational achievement and length of service are compared; it is apparent that when entry grade is held constant, the effect of length of service is greater in every case. The main effect of education is on the GS classification upon entry into federal service; promotion prospects are largely determined by length of service or by the performance and other factors that longevity in an organization implies.

It is reasonable to infer that the organizational relevance of formal educational achievements tends to fall off in the careers of public servants. The fact that some of these workers *did* qualify for their early civil-service appointments by their educational credentials does not alter a general tendency for less educated people to move ahead, presumably on the basis of their individual merits as loyal and productive workers.

Once again, the promotability argument in defense of educational requirements suffers in confrontation with the facts of manpower utilization.

The data, of course, do not prove that the schooling of better-educated workers who are bypassed by colleagues with more longevity is wasted—indeed, the data may reflect the fact that better-educated civil servants leave public service for other jobs—nor that those better-educated workers who remain with the federal government do not utilize their schooling advantage. The data on promotion rates do suggest, however, that the quality of public service, such as it is, does *not* reflect the educational credentials of the federal work force and the upward movement of its promotable, well-educated members. At the same time, these data offer no basis for strong criticism of federal employment selection policies that reduce the significance of formal degrees and diplomas through veterans' preference, competitive examinations, and other components of the government's effort to eliminate discriminatory practices.

Such conclusions, derived from the civil-service materials, are buttressed by detailed analysis of some of the experiences of one federal agency whose performance in the public interest has been of demonstrably high quality, the Federal Aviation Administration (FAA). Few organizations in the United States must so often adapt to major technological changes and to discontinuously elevated demands for service. The FAA, which is responsible for the direction and control of all flights in the United States, operates the control-tower facilities at all public airports.

With the advent of jet-powered flight, the FAA had to solve almost overnight a horrendous technical problem with essentially the same work force of air-control personnel that had handled the propeller-driven traffic of the early 1950's. Since no civilian employers have manpower needs similar to that of the FAA in this segment of its statutory responsibilities, the agency was and is obliged to train its own technicians and control personnel. The agency confronted the challenge imaginatively by hiring and training many new people and by promoting (on the basis of "operational behavior") the people it already had. Between 1956 and 1959 the agency tripled in size.[30]

In 1966 the FAA inaugurated an Executive Selection and Inventory System (ESIS), which includes information on the civil-service grade, location, type of position, age, military-reserve status, education, experience inside and outside the agency, honors and awards, executive training, and other background data on all agency employees who reach grade 14 or higher. Its purpose is to enable the FAA to identify employees who are eligible for positions at grade 15 or higher, or who may be considered for additional training opportunities. As of 1968, there were almost 4,000 people in the ESIS system. The FAA was kind enough to furnish background data on 507 men, constituting *all* the air-traffic controllers in the system who had attained grade 14 or above.[31]

This complicated job, at a high civil-service grade, might well require, not merely the details of engineering or management science or mathematics, but all the supposed "correlates" of education—a disciplined mind, for example—and the more personal qualities that education is supposed to produce—reliability, steadfastness, responsibility, ability to think quickly, motivation, etc. Yet half of these men had no formal education

[30] Mrs. Ethel Cohen, Special Assistant to the Associate Administrator for Personnel and Training, personal communication.

[31] Data were furnished as of November, 1966. All identifying information was deleted to protect the anonymity of individuals. These 507 men are not a sample but the *universe* of controllers at grade 14 or above. It should be noted that 21, or 4 per cent, of these men, whose highest grade had been GS 14 or 15, were then in grade-13 jobs. According to the FAA Personnel and Training Branch, the reason for this apparent demotion was a change in program or in duty location at the request of a man himself, not downgrading for disciplinary or other reasons. Further evidence that they had not lost esteem in the agency is the fact that they were included in ESIS, which constitutes a pool for promotion to grades higher than 14.

beyond high school, although they did undergo very rigorous on-the-job technical training given by the FAA itself.

Of the 507 men in the study, of whom 410 had attained grade 14 and 97 were grade 15, 211 (42 per cent) had no education and no management training beyond high school.[32] An additional 48 men (almost 10 per cent) had no formal academic training beyond high school but had taken executive training courses. A few of these 48 men had more than three courses of managerial training, but most had only one. Thus, more than half the men had no academic training beyond high school. Further analysis of the data revealed no pattern of differences among educational groups by the position of the men in grade 15 or grade 14. That is, neither amount of education nor managerial training was related to higher grade.

It could be argued, of course, that the possibility of reaching certain positions depends on supply and demand at particular times and places, especially in an operation as decentralized as the FAA. According to such logic, given the scarcity of highly specialized skill, the agency was restricted to "low educated" manpower and was forced to promote what it had, regardless of merit. Nevertheless, the agency has been quite satisfied with the performance of its controllers, and the public has benefited from their remarkable safety records and their capacities for administering overcrowded airports.

In addition to the FAA's extraordinary record, the honors and awards received by tower controllers can be used as a rough measure of performance. ESIS records 21 different honors and awards, six of which were included in the data available. FAA personnel administrators were extremely uncomfortable about using these awards as a measure of performance. Honors are awarded on the basis of a subjective, unstandardized assessment of a man's work by his supervisor

---

[32] For personnel purposes, the FAA assumes that all employees have the equivalent of a high-school education. Since a diploma is neither required nor recorded, some of these 211 men may conceivably have been dropouts.

(for government-wide awards) or his supervisor's manager (for specific FAA honors).[33]

The number of honors weighs barely at all in consideration of a man for promotion. The agency has better information at its disposal. Not only is each man rigorously trained for his job and for the specific geographical subsection of his air tower's jurisdiction, but he is under constant observation. Traffic controllers work by talking to pilots, and every word they say is recorded and logged. A controller's records include every "confliction"[34] that occurs under his direction.

Unfortunately, the detailed performance data on each man are not available in tabular form.[35] Consequently, since major personnel decisions in private firms (especially decisions regarding white-collar workers) are often made on the basis of judgments such as those that go into the conferring of honors here,[36] it seemed reasonable to use honors as a rough measure of performance with the FAA's reservations in mind.

Table VIII-5 shows an impressive performance; only one third of these men never received an award, and 43 per cent earned more than one. College graduates were least likely to

[33] More specifically, such honors as Quality Step Increases, Sustained Superior Performance, and Outstanding Performance Ratings are common to the total government structure and are an innate part of the review of an individual's performance on an annual basis. Each of these awards is a specific recognition of unusual performance. On the other hand, Meritorious Service Awards, Certificates of Achievement, and Special Act or Service Awards are peculiar to the FAA award structure and are generally a little more difficult to obtain. The former category includes awards bestowed by the immediate supervisor with the blessing of the next-higher echelon, whereas the latter awards are bestowed only with the approval of a board or committee at a higher level (Mrs. Ethel Cohen, personal communication).

[34] When two planes come too near each other, the occurrence is called a confliction.

[35] The agency has an "up or out" policy and is eager to promote qualified people to the "journeyman" level. With such rigorous supervision, a move up in itself is a tribute to performance.

[36] Business journals are crammed with articles on how to evaluate employee performance. The elements are often quite personal, psychological, or of the grade-school report-card "deportment" variety.

TABLE VIII-5

EDUCATION AND MANAGERIAL TRAINING OF FAA CONTROLLERS,
G.S. 14 OR ABOVE, BY NUMBER OF HONORS AND AWARDS RECEIVED

Education	Managerial Training	Honors and Awards Received, Percentage of Group				
		None	One	Two or More	Total %	Total N
No college	None	30%	27%	43%	100	210
No college	Some	41	24	35	100	49
Some college	None	31	21	48	100	182
Some college	Some	38	24	38	100	16
College graduate	None	51	13	36	100	45
Total		34%	23%	43%	100	502

have received honors; the most awards were earned by non-college graduates *without* managerial training.

Here again, the FAA's cautions about the meaning of these awards must be taken into account; not all supervisors are willing to go through the red tape necessary to obtain them for their workers. Consequently, differences in the achievement of honors may reflect the personalities of supervisors more than the qualities of the men they supervise; there is a possibility that the high-honors men worked under supervisors who were more willing to take the trouble to arrange for awards than others. Furthermore, the small number of men in the "more educated" categories means that a few supervisors could strongly affect the data. However, there is no reason to believe that supervisors' idiosyncrasies were strongly correlated with the education of their men. Members of the Personnel and Training Section nevertheless felt that, although those who received awards did in fact deserve them, many among those not so honored were equally deserving and might have received them but for their supervisors.

Apart from these reservations, it should be noted that the FAA did very well with respect to government-wide awards. Half the men were chosen at least once; more than a hundred

TABLE VIII-6
EDUCATION OF FAA CONTROLLERS, G.S. 14 OR ABOVE,
BY NUMBER OF GOVERNMENT-WIDE OUTSTANDING
PERFORMANCE AWARDS

| Education | Number of Government-wide Awards, Percentage of Group | | | | |
	None	One	Two or More	Total %	Total N
No college	51%	29%	20%	100	258
1 year of college	51	27	22	100	81
2 years of college	45	37	18	100	65
3 years of college	36	33	31	100	52
College graduate	67	20	13	100	45
Total N	50	29	21	100	501

of them, or one fifth of the total, were recognized for Outstanding Performance at least twice. The results when education is held constant (Table VIII-6) tend to mirror earlier findings: men with no more than a high-school education were just as likely to be outstanding in their on-the-job performance as those with one year of college. There *is*, however, a slight relationship with education: those with two or three years of college received more Outstanding Performance awards than did those with more or less education.

The performance of the better-educated tower controllers declines, however, when other, rarer awards are considered. Those with graduate degrees are underrepresented among the men honored for "Sustained Superior Performance," whereas those with two years of college did disproportionately well; those with no formal schooling beyond high school held their own.

When we look at "Quality Step Increases," which were awarded to only 12 per cent of the controllers, those with three or more years of college do better than those with less education (even the BA's hold their own this time), but neither of the two men who received more than one such award had attended college. There is little difference among educational groups in receiving the very rare merit-service awards and achievement certificates, but none of those with degrees received either.

In the logic of the enthusiasts of educational credentials, the FAA was "stuck" with the manpower it had. And because it was forced to train men and was unable to rely on formal credentials, the agency did not screen out men who would not have been permitted to take these positions in private industry or to undergo the relevant on-the-job training. Even if educational achievement *had* been used as a screening criterion, some of the excellent *better*-educated men would not have been hired; most of these men obtained their higher degrees only after their employment by the FAA.

Because it was "stuck" with less educated men—the expression may stick in one's craw—the FAA became a little laboratory in which the relevance of education for attainment of, and achievement in, important managerial and technical positions could be examined. Education proves not to be a factor in the daily performance of one of the most demanding decision-making jobs in America.

The FAA experience becomes even more significant in light of the fact that these positions are analogous to numerous posts in private industry, especially in the "technology industries." Many of these jobs are basically managerial, and any comparable management job in industry would be virtually inaccessible to anyone without at least a BA or BS degree, and often to those without an MA or MBA. If the requirement of technical knowledge of a highly specialized field prohibits the recruitment of managers from the outside, the FAA experience provides a compelling argument for advising technical industries, especially engineering companies, to hire without a compulsive regard for education and to promote from within. The highly technical and specialized industries that hire managers from the top and that insist on higher degrees for their engineers are exercising an irrational personnel policy. As was indicated in the earlier discussion of the rewards and evaluations accorded to more than 600 engineers and scientists, employers are not necessarily so economically efficient as the widows and orphans among their stockholders would like to believe.

It is saddening, especially in light of these findings, to report that FAA management expects that the educational attainments of future ATC's will be much higher, probably by FAA preference. They expect that increased job complexity and the introduction of automatic data processing will necessitate a knowledge of mathematics, air-transport economics, and "spatial relations"; at present the FAA is contracting with universities to teach these subjects.

Air Traffic Control Training would *still* have to be done by the FAA alone, however, and under repeated questioning they said that their desire to recruit more educated men does not reflect dissatisfaction with the performance of their present controllers. Rather, it reflects a *presumption* that ADP and other complexities will require more educated men, a desire to "keep up" with the rest of government, which they say is raising requirements, and a belief that, although educated men are not necessarily better, the increasing education of the population in general reflects invidiously on those with less education.

FAA spokesmen did express their intention of examining whether increased education actually is beneficial, once they accumulate a sufficient number of college men for comparison and their personnel records are sufficiently automated to permit tabulated comparisons of performance. An earlier effort to "build education into their testing procedures" was unsuccessful.

Assuredly, the managers of the public and military services in America are as education-conscious as those in private industry. At the same time, they must operate within the circumscriptions imposed by the realities of the labor market as well as by those that inhere in financial and public-policy decisions made in the name of government's many constituencies. These circumscriptions shape the options facing public leaders on the personnel front; willy-nilly, they must forego whatever benefits are assumed to grow directly from the use of formal educational criteria in the selection and assignment of people.

The available evidence does not prove that the restrictions on personnel policy have significant bearing on the job performance of those who do the people's work. There is, in fact, more evidence to support the proposition that educational credentials *as such* have relatively little bearing on performance; the extent to which public services function well is apparently related to other factors, including the managerial skills of those in responsible and accountable positions.

This conclusion need not be unwelcome in either educational or financial circles. Indeed, it should give heart to all who would prefer that organizations maximize their returns from the resources they are privileged to employ, as well as to those whose objections to "bureaucracy" include the charge that government agencies tend toward inflexibility in their operations and toward a dread organizational disease that, for lack of better terminology, may be called hardening of the categories.

The irony will not be lost on some that the nonrational use of formal credentials, which might be taken as a significant symptom of "bureaupathology," is more likely to be found in our great private enterprises than in our governmental apparatus. The capacity of industry leaders to temper the effect of the marketplace in an age of subsidies, tax shelters, stockpiling programs, depreciation allowances, and rulings that facilitate the deduction of fines and damages for price conspiracies as "ordinary business expenses" is undoubtedly related to the luxurious consumption of high-priced labor. As a consequence, it is the public that shops in the competitive market so favored in economists' models. It is the public's hired managers who must act the role of the entrepreneur in imaginatively combining scarce human resources.

The argument that it might be more pleasant to deal with a well-educated employee of a business firm than with his less educated peer in public service will not be persuasive to most thoughtful readers, especially not to those who have had experiences with credit offices in leading department stores, managers of auto companies who are unwilling to honor their own and their dealers' obligations under corporate warranties, insurance claims representatives, or employers who have used armed plant policemen in response to union organizing efforts.

Certainly, as the relevant chapters indicate, the writer had greater success in government than in business in getting at the problem of the utilization of educated manpower. His hopes for the future of private enterprise received no boost from his interviews about manpower with business leaders who were otherwise among the most articulate and charming people one could wish to encounter.

IX The Great Training Robbery

Of all the arguments that have been mobilized with respect to education's central place in American life, the hardest to confront are those that emphasize the "social returns," including the so-called external benefits, and the "social costs" attending education. The issues in this realm are singularly hard to frame, for they bridge empirical and philosophical questions that force a simultaneous consideration of methodology and values; such universes of discourse do not lend themselves to ready amalgamation.

Still, it is possible, without treating these major questions in detail, to pinpoint a few specific problems generated by the present-day enthusiasm regarding formal education before presenting the tentative conclusions supported by this study. First, we can pause to examine the correlates of the emphasis on education within the educational establishment itself that parallel those discussed in earlier chapters. Second, it may be useful to suggest briefly some of the implications of this emphasis for the quality of education in America. Finally, we will submit some general recommendations in the context of a few observations about what can be called liberals' responsibilities.

The Educational Establishment

In the academic year 1966–67, total expenditures for formal education in the United States were nearly $49 billion, including $32 billion for elementary and secondary education. The sums devoted to public schooling, which comprised 2.4 per cent of GNP in 1938, comprised 3.8 per cent in 1966–67.[1] Clark Kerr, formerly president of the University of California and now with the Carnegie Foundation, has recently estimated that over the next decade, expenditures on higher education alone, excluding expenditures on federally sponsored contract and grant research, "will need to rise . . . to 3 per cent of the Gross National Product,"[2] a proportion close to the proportion of the GNP currently being spent for *public* education.

An interesting aspect of these developments is that they have an immediate impact on the structure and functioning of the educational apparatus itself. This apparatus is growing by leaps and bounds and has become vulnerable to the problems of most growing systems, including consolidations calculated, like mergers, to yield economies of scale, unionization, and "bureaucratization."[3] For present purposes, however, the most interesting effect, an effect related to those generated by rapid growth, has been the expansion of demand for educated manpower within education.

Education, as was noted in the previous chapter, is the most important nondefense activity in the public sector as a field of government employment. Its growth has been accompanied by a dramatic change in the academic achievements of teachers—so dramatic that today as many as three fourths of all jobs defined as requiring college degrees are teaching jobs

[1] These and a number of other intriguing facts on education appear in a useful booklet by the Committee for Economic Development, *Innovation in Education: New Directions for the American School* (New York: Committee for Economic Development, 1968).

[2] Clark Kerr, "The Distribution of Money and Power," *The Public Interest*, XI (1968), 100.

[3] See Michael Moskow, *Teachers and Unions* (Philadelphia: University of Pennsylvania, Wharton School of Finance and Commerce Industrial Research Unit, 1966), for a fine discussion of these and related developments.

TABLE IX-1

PERCENTAGE DISTRIBUTION OF YEARS OF SCHOOL COMPLETED
BY TEACHERS,[a] BY SEX, 1950 AND 1960

Years of School Completed	1950			1960		
	Males	Females	Total	Males	Females	Total
8 years or less	3.2	1.6	2.0	0.8	0.5	0.5
1–3 years of high school	2.4	1.0	1.3	1.2	1.4	1.3
High-school graduate	5.5	5.0	5.2	3.5	4.6	4.3
1–3 years of college	12.7	29.3	25.1	7.8	22.3	18.2
College graduate	76.2	63.1	66.4	86.7	71.2	75.7
Number (in thousands)	(287.9)	(842.2)	(1130.1)	(476.9)	(1205.5)	(1682.4)

[a] Includes elementary- and secondary-school teachers plus "teachers not elsewhere classified"; excludes college instructors and professors.
SOURCE: 1950 Census, *Occupational Characteristics* (Special Report P-E No. 1B), Table 10; 1960 Census, *Occupational Characteristics* (Subject Report PC (2)-7A), Table 9.

(see Chapter III). Not all teachers have such academic achievements, of course, but the figures are impressive (Table IX-1).

Meanwhile, the number of teachers increased by almost 50 per cent from 1950 to 1960, a rate of increase much higher than that sustained by the work force, which grew about 15 per cent in the same decade.[4] One can conclude, accordingly, that the mounting demand for education feeds in no small part upon itself. And this conclusion leads to the further conclusion that an examination of the correlates of the educational achievements of teachers is as important as the examination of these correlates among the populations considered in earlier chapters.

[4] For more extensive data on the educational achievements of teachers, see John K. Folger and Charles B. Nam, *Education and the American Population, 1960 Census Monograph* (Washington: U.S. Department of Commerce, Bureau of the Census, 1968), pp. 84–86.

Not many reasonable people are skeptical about the utility or relevance of undergraduate degrees for teachers in the nation's schools. But we might ask about the relevance of the postgraduate training these educators pursue.

Consider that it is not at all unusual for school systems to pay differential salaries according to the educational achievements of their teachers. In addition, and to encourage them to undertake further studies, teachers are generally awarded salary increases for academic work pursued after hours or during their summer vacations and sabbatical leaves.

These personnel practices may redound to the advantage of pupils, but there is no evidence that relates their performance to their teachers' educational achievements. There is some evidence, however, that teachers, like employees elsewhere, tend to become dissatisfied with their occupational achievements and to look to greener economic pastures. Data from the postcensal study conducted in 1962 by the National Opinion Research Center and the National Science Foundation on nearly 4,000 teachers are illustrative.[5] In a comparison of the positions held by these teachers in 1960 and 1962, there is no evidence that better-educated teachers are more likely to move out of education than are less educated teachers of a given age or level of teaching. Indeed, this type of teacher turnover was negatively related to educational achievement over this very short period.

There is strong evidence, however, that over a longer period both elementary and secondary teachers are less likely to stay in teaching as they move up the educational ladder (see Table IX-2). It is a matter of speculation whether this is a good thing, whether school systems benefit from the pat-

[5] These data were made available by Professor Seymour Warkov, of Teachers College, formerly of NORC. They are more fully exploited in Harold Oaklander, "The Career Perspective of Teachers" (Doctoral dissertation, Columbia University Graduate School of Business, in progress under the writer's direction).

TABLE IX-2

PERCENTAGE OF TEACHERS WHO HAD HELD THREE OR MORE POSITIONS,
BY EDUCATION, SEX, AND SCHOOL LEVEL, 1962

	Education			
	Not a College Graduate	College Graduate	Some Graduate School	Master's Degree
Males				
Elementary	37 (30)ª	17 (41)	22 (117)	40 (114)
Secondary	36 (76)	24 (153)	28 (343)	38 (422)
Females				
Elementary	54 (411)	40 (469)	41 (254)	48 (176)
Secondary	52 (71)	40 (268)	48 (198)	50 (227)

ª The numbers in parentheses represent the base on which percentages were calculated.

SOURCE: Oaklander, *op. cit.*

terns implied by the table. It is probable, however one evaluates the results, that if communities wish to reward their teachers' loyalty, they are not conspicuously successful; the table implies that systems of salaries for teachers enhance the labor-market potentialities of teachers at least as much as they serve the interests intended.

Other data, collected in 1962 by the Institute of Administrative Research, Teachers College, on three suburban school systems bordering New York City and Philadelphia, have also been analyzed in the detailed study by Harold Oaklander cited above. They serve to amplify the patterns observed in the postcensal materials.

There is no evidence in these data that the more educated teachers in the three systems are more likely to wish to continue as classroom teachers. The data can be broken down in a variety of ways—by sex, by age, and by the school levels on which these 933 teachers work.

TABLE IX-3
PERCENTAGE OF TEACHERS HAVING HELD POSITIONS IN MORE THAN ONE SCHOOL SYSTEM, BY SEX AND EDUCATION

	Education	
	Bachelor's Degree	Master's Degree or Higher
Males	16 (85)ᵃ	25 (238)
Females	20 (359)	36 (251)

ᵃ The numbers in parentheses represent the base on which percentages were calculated.
SOURCE: Oaklander, *op. cit.*

When the teachers are grouped according to whether they have acquired at least a master's degree, we find that 32 per cent of those with postgraduate degrees want to leave classroom teaching, compared to 25 per cent of those who hold only a bachelor's degree. Male elementary and junior-high-school teachers and female senior-high-school teachers who wish to move away from the classroom into other educational jobs, or out of education entirely, account for the sizable difference between the two groups.

The teachers in these three systems are not unlike those in the much larger postcensal study in that those with relatively high educational achievements are more likely to have had jobs in school systems other than the one in which they were employed at the time of the survey (Table IX-3).

Although there are many forces that result in the occupational transitions in these tables—the jobs of spouses and the family plans of female teachers come readily to mind—the educational differences are at the very least suspiciously parallel to the other patterns that have been identified throughout the present study.

The Quality of Education

Inner-city school critics are much more concerned with other aspects of performance than with those that reflect the dissatisfactions of teachers. They would remind us that the deterioration of urban education has been unaffected by the rising educational credentials of teachers. While turnover rates may in part reflect teachers' quests for rewards commensurate with their educational achievements, these achievements are viewed skeptically by many Americans, both in and out of city school districts.

This skepticism gains some force through these data. By emphasizing teachers' academic credentials to the degree we do in America, we substantially subvert the reform of programs in the nation's schools and departments of education. An incentive and salary system linked to academic credentials not only may backfire, as the turnover data strongly imply, but may serve to subsidize teachers' colleges by guaranteeing them large numbers of clients. Therefore, these institutions are under little pressure to institute much-needed changes in their efforts to train educators.

The poor and their stymied young are not the only ones, of course, who complain about education in America. The numbers of more privileged groups may not match the volume or character of their protest; they may not be proportionate to the hideousness and perversions in education to which they point, but there is plentiful evidence that youths who are favored with an opportunity to attend "better" schools at all levels are less than happy with their experience.

Student demonstrations like those at Columbia, Cornell, and Harvard rattle many citizens on and off campus, just as the uprisings in some urban high schools and the "liberated" behavior of suburban adolescents offend the sensibilities and upset the equilibria of whole communities. These developments should not distract attention, however, from the objects of the students' wrath and the substance of young people's complaints that inform (if they do not precisely illuminate) the logic of their behavior. Their teachers, perhaps surprisingly, do sometimes pinpoint the issues, though with fewer obscurantist trappings. Witness the following formulation:

> . . . as Americans move into the end of the twentieth century, there is one institution which can no longer afford the luxury of waiting to see how the story turns out, and that is the institution of education itself. Not simply because education has a stake in the notion that self-consciousness is a good thing but because education, especially at its higher reaches, now plays a leading part in the plot. . . .
>
> What troubles American education today is the simple fact that it has no choice between [two] simple alternatives. It must meet both demands. It must serve power and yet make that power humane. Whether it can or not is at the bottom of what troubles American education today.[6]

This speaks to the point that many young people seek to make when they protest government contracts with universities and the irrelevance of contemporary education. They charge that education focuses on vocational placement in a society of buttondown personalities and grey-flannel mouths, competing to breathe the technicians' polluted air, to drive the engineers' beached whales on crowded cement ribbons that choke the planners' cities. Education mirrors a society, they argue, in which liberation is confused with "upward mobility," and in which human relationships are confounded with the ritual behavior of the polite middle class. One may conjure up an image of an educated community in which the inanities of cocktail-party patter regularly pass for conversa-

---

[6] John William Ward, "The Trouble with Higher Education," *The Public Interest* (No. 4, Spring 1966), p. 88.

tion, in which clam dip serves as social cement, in which work is a job and not labor, crabgrass is the evil goddess to whom one kneels in Sunday terror, spiritual values are high-proof, neutral, and pure grain, and suburban husbands are handymen with sex privileges.

These charges are not lightly dismissed, as educable teachers realize and as most parents of teenagers are obliged to learn. It is the adult culture, especially its educated culture, the young argue, that has most truly gone to pot.

Education, Class Barriers, and the Liberal Creed

The defenders of the educational establishment point out that things could be worse and that critics have overstated their case. Education, they assert, produces thoughtful citizens and material well-being; the economic benefits to the society are accordingly stressed and linked, by assertion, to social welfare. But surely, in a discussion of education, the definition of social welfare must go beyond aggregated tallies of material benefits to include the matter of education's role in the distribution of social product. And when the issues are thus joined, the defense is less compelling.

Educational credentials have become the new property in America. Our nation, which has attempted to make the transmission of real and personal property difficult, has contrived to replace it with an inheritable set of values concerning degrees and diplomas which will most certainly reinforce the formidable class barriers that remain, even without the right within families to pass benefices from parents to their children.

As a number of my colleagues have suggested, employers can derive benefits from the employment of better-educated workers that outweigh the pathological correlates of "excessive" ed-

ucation; after all, the intent was only to open up the nar-
rower economic issues. But the use of educational credentials
as a screening device effectively consigns large numbers of
people, especially young people, to a social limbo defined
by low-skill, no-opportunity jobs in the "peripheral labor
market."[7]

Barriers against greater mobility are not made less imposing
by public policies that reinforce the access to formal education of middle- and upper-income youngsters through sub-
sidy and subsidy-like arrangements. Today, tax-supported
and tax-assisted universities are full of nutant spirits from
families whose incomes are well above those of the average
taxpayers. The personal advantages to those who hold academic credentials are sufficiently well known that the majority of Americans do not even pause to question the TV
spots or subway posters that warn of the lifetime hazards
facing "dropouts."

If the barriers to mobility are not fully visible to the disin-
herited, poverty warriors have been armed with weapons to
subdue the poor in skirmishes against the "disadvantaged"
which have distracted attention from a much-needed war
against poverty. Substantial funds from that war chest have
been consumed by educational mercenaries who campaign
against the personal—which is to say educational—deficiencies
of the youthful poor. Foot-long ads addressed to "educational
technologists" offer grand salaries and extensive benefits to
induce men and women (many of those who respond are
public-school teachers) to enroll in the legions who will train
impoverished youths in encampments across the land, financed
by profitable cost-plus contracts.[8]

During the life of the office of Economic Opportunity and

---

[7] See Dean Morse, *The Peripheral Worker* (New York: Columbia University Press, 1969).

[8] See Ivar Berg and Marcia Freedman, "Job Corps: A Business Bonanza,"
Christianity and Crisis (May 31, 1965).

the thousand community-action programs it spawned, unemployment rates among the nation's less educated have
dropped; black workers had an unemployment rate of 6.8 per
cent in 1968—"the lowest," according to the Department of
Labor, "since 1953."[9] But it is not at all clear what portion of
this gain—modest as it is—is attributable to the war against
poverty. The Labor Department's estimate that "the sharp
Vietnam buildup began, largely unexpectedly, at the very
time the economy was already being propelled toward full
employment by surging civilian demand" must be balanced
against its own statement that "in the two years after mid-
1965, increased defense expenditures generated a total of 1.8
million jobs—some 700,000 in the Armed Forces and about a
million in private industry."[10] Whatever can be said in favor
of our wars, it is unsettling that they are among the significant
mergers of our time.

The quality of public education available to the poor and
near-poor is almost uniformly low, a fact that contributes increasingly to the visibility of the barrier between the haves
and the have-nots. For the have-nots, especially black Americans, there is a special pain in all this, for they are underrepresented in the policy-making councils that have decreed the
frightful mess in urban education and the segregated style of
American living and learning, but they are overrepresented
among those who suffer the penalties in foxholes overseas and
ratholes at home.

At least as sharp a pain must afflict some thoughtful liberals
in America. For them formal education has been the equili-
brating mechanism in a progressing industrial democracy
that has been relatively free of class conflict. It was the liberal
who helped to sell America on education and who saw in ed-

[9] *Manpower Report of the President* (Washington: U.S. Government
Printing Office, 1969), p. 23. White unemployment rates were 3.2 per cent.
Ibid., p. 44.
[10] *Ibid.*, p. 25.

ucation the means by which merit might ultimately conquer unearned privilege. He must now acknowledge that he is the defender of a most dubious faith. For while he struggles from the edges of hard-earned privilege to help the poor, he must live off these privileges in the education of his own children.

Consider, in this context, that over one third of all school-age children in New York City, many of them the sons and daughters of earnest liberals, attend private and parochial schools.[11] It is at least ideologically convenient for the parents of these children to champion the cause of the neighborhood school and the decentralization of desperately sick urban public-school programs. The serious question of whether this makes educational and political sense may be effectively begged in favor of a willingness to "allow others" the control *they* have over their children's school experience.[12]

The position that such reforms will reverse educational inequities does put a good face on their ruggedly individualistic pursuit of their own narrow self-interest; it may be doubted whether the ragged individuals thereby left to fend for themselves will necessarily benefit from this quaint version of egalitarianism. The middle-class children of liberal and conservative parents in silk-stocking districts are doubly blessed, of course, with relatively good public schools and a self-serving ideology about the seemingly neutral principle of the neighborhood school that has now become an article of faith for many inner-city dwellers. These desperate people have gained the ideological support—and sometimes the financial support—of progressive whites, many of whom are masters at converting liberal principles into a tasteful though

11 David Rogers, *110 Livingston Street* (New York: Random House, 1968), pp. 56, 59.

12 Private-school parents, of course, may point out that their control over their children's school experience is limited to choice of school—not by any means an unlimited choice at that—since the demand for private-school services has fostered a certain indifference reminiscent of the public-school pathologies in large cities.

distracting pragmatism. Since the logics in defense of urban educational reforms are presented only less delectably by Southern politicians, the long-run advantages of such tinkering will unquestionably depend in part on the success of reformers in demonstrating that they do not mean simply to raise the hopes of their repressed protagonists. Such a demonstration must take account of the credentials barriers and the employment levels that help to sustain them; again, the education-employment nexus becomes strategically important.

Conclusion

The results of the present study do not give much weight to the economic argument in its detail, although it would be foolish to deny that education is involved in the nation's capacity to produce goods and services. No benefit would accrue from reviewing the detailed findings in this concluding chapter. Let us state, however, that they give grounds for doubting that it is useful to regard education in America within a simplified framework in which a person's *years of schooling* are taken as a significant measure; schools are too diverse and people too differentiated to permit the routine and automatic confusion of the morals, motives, and capabilities of the licensed with their licenses. The experience with marriages in Western society may illustrate the point.

Another general conclusion from the data must be that we could profitably and sensibly redirect our educational investments in order to improve primary and secondary public education. It is consistent with the observations in preceding chapters that America should be doing a far better job in assuring that *all* of her people reach adult life with twelve years of quality training and education. Employers, for example, indicate that their educational requirements reflect their dissatisfaction with what public education is accomplishing. Added expenditures for higher education, which already constitutes 34 per cent of direct educational outlays, is not likely to change all this.

Within the educational establishment there is further room for redirection.

> The missing link in education is development research as it is practiced in industry. . . . Though there is great need for more basic research in education, there is an immediate demand for more extensive developmental work which will evaluate and apply the findings of research and demonstrate their practical worth. At present only 10 to 12 per cent of the funds expended on educational research and development are devoted to development.[13]

It would also be desirable from all points of view if those who failed to take full advantage of their educational opportunities in their youth had a second chance, after discovering themselves and developing the attitudes that serve the learning process, in a system of adult education. Under present circumstances, life-long consequences stem from decisions made by, for, and against youths. And it may be questioned whether a citizen should suffer all his life with the disabilities that come of having been exposed, for example, to a poor grade-school experience, where "functional illiteracy" paves the way for disenchantment, delinquency, or deprivation.

Education needs to be reformed in America by striking a balance between "too much" for some and "not enough" for others. The tendency on the part of employers to raise educational requirements *without careful assessments of their needs, in both the short and the long run,* can benefit neither managers nor the system they extol.

This purposeless credential consciousness further handicaps

[13] Committee for Economic Development, *op. cit.,* p. 30.

education, especially higher education, in the pursuit of its promise to liberate people and to help preserve for a society its better traditions and commitments. This part of our cultural heritage is already in danger of being obscured by a growing materialism, stifled by know-nothing "status politics" and radical rightism, and weakened by the radical, disenchanted Left.

There is no escaping the fact that in America the political and social wellbeing of the individual are bound up with his economic opportunities. It is therefore a matter of great moment to the society whether the economic argument in favor of education takes far more account of the complexities involved in measuring the relationships among abilities, educational achievements, and job requirements. The efforts presented in the present volume give abundant support to the position that the issues involved in these relationships have not been adequately joined and that a more differentiated line of analysis needs to be considered in framing public policy toward education. Policies calculated to generate job opportunities for a growing population would seem to deserve higher priority than those designed to rationalize, by their stress on education, the considerable difficulties imposed on those without academic credentials.

At the same time, the data give reason for concern about the personal wellbeing of the growing numbers who do not find that their investments in education are earning them the rewards they were taught to anticipate. The political consequences of latent discontent are not necessarily less threatening to democratic institutions than those of the noisier versions of American dissaffection.

Finally, it is appropriate to call attention to the role of the American academic community in the processes by which credentials have come to loom so significantly in the lives of their fellow citizens. A Columbia University colleague has put one major aspect of the matter well:

Is it not dangerously presumptuous to insist, despite our lack of understanding about the contribution of college schooling to occupational performance, that nevertheless, all professionals must pay a toll to the schools and the teachers? University administrators and college professors have been put into a position that all too closely resembles the old robber barons on the Rhine. They exact not just coin from those who wish passage to professional employment but also the more valuable asset, time—four to eight years of students' lives. . . .

For those who want to do more than pass through to a career . . . college has much to offer for its cost. The offering takes the form of perspectives, understanding, and insights rather than lucrative techniques and productive skills. . . . [However] not all persons find such an education to their taste or in their interests; some may wish to pursue a career as immediately as possible, postponing until later, or doing without, the contribution education might make to their lives. At present, choice is denied. Entrance to a career is through college, where schooling all too often is masked as education. Would not the colleges, teachers, students, and those who look forward to professional careers be better served if other entry ways were open, available, and used?[14]

It is by no means clear that Professor Kuhn's questions are easily answered, but they deserve the attention of educators who manage the sluice gates that determine so substantially the directions of the nation's manpower flows.

Another major aspect of academics' role in credential-making catches them up in the apparatuses that maintain the status quo with respect to the distribution of America's wealth. Data presented earlier call attention to the "class bias" that attends the economics of education, a development that exacerbates the increasingly conservative implications of education in America.

[14] James W. Kuhn, "The Misuse of Education: The Problem of Schooling for Employment," speech presented at the inauguration of Dr. Gordon C. Bjork as President of Linfield College, McMinnville, Oregon, May 20, 1969.

The significance of this development gains additional force in a study of "the methodology for estimating the benefits and costs of higher education for a state, and . . . the relationship of these benefits and costs to legislative policy," by Professors Hansen and Weisbrod, of the University of Wisconsin.[15] Using data on the California system of higher education, the authors, distinguished students of the economics of education, report:

> Public subsidies for higher education in California tend to go disproportionately to students from relatively high-income families and are received in quite different amounts by people even within given income classes. Almost 40 per cent of the student-age population receives no subsidy whatsoever, while a relatively small group receives very substantial subsidies. Whether this pattern of subsidy distribution is consistent with the social objective of equality of educational opportunity is certainly open to question.[16]

The academic community may, of course, uphold high standards for admission to their institutions, both public and private, on the basis of hallowed academic principles. The fact is, however, that the "educationally disadvantaged" students will *not* receive credentials for the well-paying jobs in the economy to which high academic standards and degrees stand in problematic relation.

Perhaps the academic community owes it to the losers to re-examine the talents and capabilities of the considerable population groups to which current educational measures, tests, and examinations do not attend. Perhaps such a charge relates to the matter of "relevance," about which more is said than done on America's comfortable campuses these days. One's

---

[15] W. Lee Hansen and Burton A. Weisbrod, *Benefits, Costs and Finance of Public Higher Education* (Chicago: Markham Publishing Co., 1969), p. vii.

[16] *Ibid.*, p. 84.

own experiences as an educator are not heartening, but pessimism in respect to reforms that would be responsive to the needs of losers is a most inappropriately self-serving emotion for the innumerable subsidized tenants of America's academic mansions.

Index

Ability, college entrance and, 102
Abramoff, Michael, 88n
Absenteeism, educational achievement, and, 88, 98–100
Airman Classification Battery, 148
Alchian, Armen A., 69n
Alienation, 105–6
American Airlines, 100–101
Anderson, Adolph V., 155
Appet, Hugh, 39n
Aptitude tests; see Tests, aptitude
Armed Forces, educational achievement in, 145–60
Army Classification Battery, 157–58
Army Classification Tests, 148
Army General Classification Test, 41
Attitude; see Job dissatisfaction; Worker attitude
Automatic data processing, job requirements and, 174
Awards by Federal Aviation Administration (FAA), educational achievement and, 169–73

Bakke, E. Wright, 4
Balogh, Thomas, 35–36
Baumol, William, 34n
Bausch and Lomb Optical Company, 100
Becker, Gary, 9, 27n, 29, 32n, 40n, 101–2
Bell, Daniel, 106n, 107n
Bell, H. M., 42n
Berg, Ivar, 77n, 186n

Blau, Peter, 62n
Blaug, M., 27n
Blauner, Robert, 120n, 122–42
Blue-collar workers, 87–90, 121–42
Bowen, William G., 24n, 25n, 30–31
Bowman, Mary Jean, 9n, 25n, 26n
Bray, Douglas, 153n
Brockaw, Leland, 149–52
Bullock, Robert, 116
Bureaucratization, measuring of, 138–39

Campus disturbances, 183–85
Cantril, Hadley, 110n
Caplowitz, David, 135n
Cassell, Frank, 45n
Centers, Richard, 110n
Chamberlain, Neil, 20n, 53n
Chandler, Margaret, 72n
Child Labor Amendment to Constitution, 5n
Civil service: educational achievement in, 161; promotion in, 162–79
Class: and education, 185–89; see also Socioeconomic class; Status inconsistency
Cohen, Ethel, 168n, 170n
Cofer, C. N., 154n
College entrance: and ability, 102; and socioeconomic class, 102
College graduates, number of, 1
College student military service deferments, 6–7
Connors, Ralph P., 108n
Cooley, William V., 102n